The Tibetan Book of Meditation

The Tibetan Book
of Meditation

Lama Christie McNally

DOUBLEDAY

New York London Toronto Sydney Auckland

CD

DOUBLEDAY

Published in the United States by Doubleday Religion,
an imprint of the Crown Publishing Group,
a division of Random House, Inc., New York.
www.doubleday.com

DOUBLEDAY and the DD colophon are registered trademarks
of Random House, Inc.

Library of Congress Cataloging-in-Publication Data
McNally, Christie.
The Tibetan book of meditation / Christie McNally.
p. cm.
1. Meditation—Buddhism. 2. Buddhism—China—Tibet—Doctrines. I. Title.
BQ7805.M38 2009
294.3'4435—dc22
2009012694

ISBN 978-0-385-51815-4

PRINTED IN THE UNITED STATES OF AMERICA

1 3 5 7 9 10 8 6 4 2

First Edition

For

Nanhee ~

With love,
Lara Christie

The Tibetan Book of Meditation

Contents

So you want to learn how to meditate.
Come, let me show you
the way.

Chaktsel

Bowing Down

I know you. I had a vision of you deep in meditation, and I reached out to you, I planted a seed, and now I have the good fortune to be able to speak to you here, through this book. My deepest wish is to share with you the incredible kindness passed down to me by all my holy Teachers.

I have been so very lucky. I have had the very best of Teachers guiding me since day one. Let me just take a moment here, to recognize some of them, and give you a small picture of who is speaking through me.

First and foremost is my heart's Teacher and Guide, Geshe Michael Roach, Seer of Emptiness, holder of the Truth, lifelong companion, my very life, without whom nothing at all would be possible, for any goodness that I have is simply Him poured into me.

Holy Lama, I press my head to the lotus beneath your holy feet.

Then, in order of appearance...

My dear mom, love itself, who taught me how to step into the other person's shoes, and who showed me again and again the high practice of giving one's life for the sake of another.

My dad, heart so big, showing me the great honor of serving people tirelessly and joyfully.

Greg Linington, noble prince, who opened the door to the highest path.

Mark Neack, my other side, who took me to a different world, and taught me how to create.

Shri Sharon Gannon, fearless one, and David Life Ji, gentle soul, who lured me to India—the Land of the Realized Ones.

The monk formerly known as Guy Rom, a young Buddha who emanated to encourage me as I sat in my very first meditations.

Venerable Karen Valham, patient one, hidden master, my first formal teacher of the dharma in this life.

Khen Rinpoche Geshe Lobsang Tharchin, the Frightener Himself, who tirelessly passed on this great lineage to us crazy westerners.

Venerable Robina Courtin, powerful and kind, who came and held my hand.

Sermey Geshe Thubten Rinchen, mind vast as the sky itself, who pushed my reasoning beyond its normal capacity, and who guided me to the left.

Gyume Khensur Rinpoche, peacemaker, who granted me the secret.

Lama Zopa Rinpoche, dearest of spiritual friends, giving the highest of advices and always there to call on in need.

Geshe Lobsang Thardo, great mother, master of guru yoga, kindly hitting me over the head as needed.

The Wise and accomplished Gene Smith, secret yogi, who travels deep into the realm of mind.

His Holiness the Dalai Lama, Loving Eyes, who gave us all the priceless gift of opening these teachings to the world, and who gave me the answer to my prayers.

Pandiji Kanheya Sharma, Lord of the Dance, my doorway into Kashi, who offered me fire and water.

Swami Swaroopananda Ji, ancient sage, who teaches me the source of bliss.

All the teachers of the Indian lineage, who showed me another view of the very same path: Dharma Mittra Ji, Shri Pattabhi Jois, and Lady Ruth Lauer, to name a few.

Trace Murphy, enlightened editor, who believed in me; and Jon Sheer, who fell from the sky to make it happen.

Finally, my sweet angel students at Diamond Mountain University, my purpose, endlessly pointing me in the right direction, and endlessly pushing me higher. Particularly Rob Ruisinger, my design master; and Alistair Holmes, James Connor, and Ian Thorson, who helped me write this book.

I am ever thankful for all my holy Teachers both present and past, for planting such incredible seeds.

But perhaps that is not quite all, for in calling me to write this book, you have become my Teacher—pushing me one step further on the path to the final goal. And for that, I am grateful, and I bow down to you.

1

A Bit about the Author

Life is strange. For 21 years of my life, I had never heard of meditation, and Tibet was just a small dot on the map. Then I went East and everything shifted.

Imagine—you open up a book on Tibetan meditation, and written inside is an exact description of the visualization you used to picture as a child as you fell asleep.

Imagine—you meet someone for the very first time, and yet your heart is so full of joy to be seeing them again that you burst into tears.

Imagine—you are led through the corridors of a Tibetan monastery, into a small dark room, where one very old monk you've never seen before laughs at you in recognition, bows to you and makes you offerings.

Imagine—you have never meditated before, so you sit down to try, and are instantly transported to someplace...higher.

Imagine—you are staring into the eyes of your heart Teacher, when their face starts to change; into the face of One you knew long long ago.

I had never really thought about rebirth before, but as the evidence of my past lives quickly started piling up in front of me, I became a bit more interested. Who was I really? Was I just a girl from California, or was I also some great Tibetan yogi meditator Lama?

This is not the first time for any of us—we have all been here before and we're all more than we seem. We have been traveling this path together now for many lives. Things happened very quickly for me after I met these teachings, for they say all it takes is a trigger, just a tiny drop of water, and then all the seeds in your mind open like a flower and you are transported to the place on your path where you left off in your previous life. This is certainly what happened to me, and I am hoping this book can be such a trigger for you.

In any case, just a few short years later, and I found myself entering into one of the most rigorous practices you can do—what they call a *Great Retreat*, where you take yourself to an isolated place and meditate there for 3 years, 3 months, and 3 days. No talking, no seeing anyone else, no outside communication of any kind—just a lone explorer in the deepest oceans of the mind.

(If this sounds romantic to you, like something you'd like to try, I would advise starting with a week. Being alone with your own mind can be...challenging, at times.)

There were six of us, and we made our way out to a remote corner in the Arizona desert—a place where no human had ever lived, a place where the coyotes and mountain lions still reigned.

We ordered little round huts from Mongolia called "yurts"— wooden poles stacked together and covered in felt and canvas, with a glass dome at the top for light.

We found three attendants willing to come out and stay with us, to bring us food and water twice a day, and then we built little fences around our yurts with a box on one side, so our caretaker could drop these things off without ever seeing us.

And there we stayed, cut off from the entire world, from March 3, 2000 to June 6, 2003.

How to explain to you all that happened inside my mind during this time? It was beautiful, it was powerful, it was extremely difficult, it was humbling and heart-opening, it was my doorway to the truth.

There are no words to describe it. But one thing I can tell you. The art of meditation is a powerful tool. It is a method you can use to change your whole world. And I pray that I can share a little of what I've learned with you.

2
The Lineage

There is a long tradition of meditation in Tibet. In all the world, it is the Tibetan people who have really mastered the vast realm of the mind. In this particular subject, they are light-years ahead of the greatest western scientists. The great meditators of Tibet are known for their miraculous feats of telepathy, and it is said that through the sheer power of their mind they can control the weather, heal the sick, and even fly in the sky. While you may or may not believe all of this, still we must all acknowledge there is something special about the Tibetan people. We need look no further than the present Dalai Lama—who has dedicated his life to peace, and who travels the world teaching people how to love each other—to figure out that perhaps there is something we should learn from them.

It all started around 750AD, when a few great Indian Lamas braved the long trek across the Himalayas to come and teach the high art of meditation to the Tibetan people. At that time Tibet was quite a rural area, made up mostly of farmers and nomadic yak herders. But these simple folk took the teachings to heart, and made them their own, and Tibet grew into the rich, high culture we see today.

There was one great Lama from India in particular who is known for bringing the teachings of meditation to Tibet. His name is Master Kamalashila. While he was in Tibet teaching, he wrote a short guidebook on how to meditate, and this book became the classic treatise on meditation instruction—a work which is the very foundation of all Tibetan meditation practice to this day.

The truth of his teachings struck a fire inside of the Tibetan people, and one by one they went off into caves to put them into practice. People like the famous Milarepa, who is known for the 100,000 songs he wrote about his practice; or his student, Gampopa, who started the famous Mahamudra meditation lineage, to name a few. There they each came to a deep, experiential understanding of these teachings, which they then passed on to others. And so the lineage was passed down unbroken from teacher to student, each new meditator adding his or her own insightful commentary.

Because of this, now we have literally thousands of Tibetan texts which illuminate for us what it is to meditate, and how to do it, and why. The only problem? They're in Tibetan! The great majority are as yet untranslated, and though some western scholars are working very hard to remedy this, it will take another 150 years to complete the job.

Thus the birth of this book. This book is a synthesis of all the great Tibetan commentaries on meditation, starting from Master Kamalashila and continuing up to modern day Lamas, as it was passed down to me by my holy Teachers. And so the lineage continues—from India, to Tibet, and on to the lands of the West, in an unbroken chain straight to you.

3

Why Meditate?

There are so many reasons why people meditate. Some people say it gives them a more peaceful mind. That's true. Others will tell you it makes the mind really sharp and creative, so you can accomplish more things. This is also true. And a few people say they just love how it feels.

Once you dive below the surface, you will discover a beautiful, crystal clear place—like a diamond hidden beneath the rubble. It is your own mind, uncovered. And you can't even imagine now the amazing things you can do with it.

Modern scientists tell us we are only using a tiny fraction of our brains. What would it be like to learn how to wake up the rest of it? It is completely possible, if you learn how to meditate.

Want to increase your IQ? Meditate. Want to be more creative? Meditate. Want to be a more peaceful person? Meditate.

All these things do come if you meditate, but they are really only by-products: something that comes automatically as you strive for a higher goal. There are much deeper reasons to learn how to meditate.

Tibetans say we have only just begun the process of awakening— that we still have quite a way to go in our evolutionary process. And it has nothing to do with building spaceships or computers. The next step in our evolution takes place within.

We were born with this incredible potential, but it mostly lies dormant inside us. We are like baby birds still enclosed within the egg, completely unaware of this vast open sky above us that could be ours. We think this is all there is to life, confined to a body and mind which limit both our vision and our activity. We need to learn how to crack open the shell and break free and fly.

And if you think about it, perhaps you have always sensed this to be true. Perhaps you can feel this constant subtle yearning in your heart for something higher. We were not brought here just to eat and sleep and make babies and die. No, your life was meant to be far more. You were meant for greatness. And perhaps I can show you the way.

I.

Ngenjung:
The Need to Get Out

4

Broken

The Tibetans say we live in a broken realm, and that only by learning the high art of meditation can we learn how to fix it.

What exactly do they mean by "broken?"

When was the first time you realized that life doesn't have a happy ending? Perhaps it was the day you learned your aunt's cancer wasn't going to get any better, or perhaps it was when your one true love broke up with you to be with someone else. Sooner or later, you figure it out. This life, it is painful.

Look around. Everyone you see is like you—struggling, searching for some kind of tiny, temporary happiness to hold onto. But it's a useless exercise, for in the end as we take our last breaths, everything we love will be ripped away from us—our friends, our family, our home, our things, and even our own body.

We all know this. We try our very best to ignore it. Focus on the good things right? But as we get older, and our bodies start to wear out, and our friends and family start to slip away from us, the inevitable end becomes harder and harder to ignore. We will lose it all.

Some people will tell you not to worry about all that—just enjoy life while it lasts. But there's a problem with that too, for even temporary happiness eludes us. We are constantly striving to get some thing, or person, or position that we think will make us happy. And then, if we actually get it, we are still dissatisfied. Why? What makes it so impossible to be happy?

Sure, we get glimpses—moments of joy in our lives that encourage us, that keep us struggling for more. The sleeping face of a child, the beauty of a sunset, a secret shared between just the two of you. But they are few and far between. And they always end. Why can't we ever hold onto them?

We don't question this because it is the only thing we have ever known. "That's just the way life is." But what if that wasn't necessarily true? What if there was a way to make the joyful moments last forever? What if there was a way not to lose everything you love in the end? What if "the way life is" was just a big mistake—if this particular realm we live in just had some kind of fatal flaw, a flaw that we could learn to fix?

What if you had the power to mold reality itself? If there was a door you could walk through, that led to endless bliss for both you and the ones you love?

For Tibetans, this is the real goal of meditation. And even if there is only a tiny possibility in your mind that these things could really happen, it is worth a try. After all, what have you got to lose?

5

A Path to the End of Pain

It's hard to think about the downside of life. Our mind just doesn't want to go there. But before we can go about changing our lives or the world, we first must come to the realization that there is something amiss about them—something that needs to be fixed. For if we are in a mindset where we think everything is fine, then we will never want to go through the rigorous process of deconstructing our world or ourselves. Nobody who was fine with the way the world worked would ever question it. Questioning is uncomfortable. It challenges everything we hold to be true.

We need to get back to that childlike state of mind, where we are looking at the world as if it were brand new, to ask once again those questions that children ask and adults stop asking. Questions like: "Why is there pain?"

So simple, yet so profound.

We have spent our whole adult lives cultivating the art of blocking out pain, pretending it doesn't exist. But in order to travel this path— the path to the end of pain—we must begin by looking at *this* life's pain in the face.

I remember quite vividly the first moment I truly understood the suffering nature of this life.

I moved to New York City for college when I was seventeen, and ended up staying there for ten years. I shared an apartment in the East Village with a woman named Lisa and her two cats. This is about Lisa's cats. If you have ever lived with an animal in your house, you know how they quickly become like family to you. Every day when I came home from work the cats would meet me at the door. And I would pet them and give them a snack and take care of them and try to make them happy. And they in turn would rub up against me and purr and tell me how much they loved me. It was nice.

One day I came home from work, and the cats were there at the door as usual, but when I stepped inside to say hello, the cat named Max froze, as if he were made of stone. He made one loud hacking sound, and then he toppled over on his side. I rushed over to him, and realized that he was no longer breathing. Panic set in my heart. What do I do?

I took him in my arms and called 911. They gave me the address of the nearest animal hospital. It was fifty blocks away. I ran out the door with Max in my arms, sobbing.

Some nice stranger hailed me a cab. The cab driver did his very best to get me there as quickly as possible, speaking consoling words now and then, but it was fifty blocks during rush hour traffic in Manhattan, and little Max still wasn't breathing. I felt so helpless.

I burst through the doors of the hospital, into a waiting room full of people with animals in their laps who all looked healthy, and they all stared at me, and then someone in a white coat came up and took him from my arms, and took me to a quiet room to cry in private. About fifteen minutes later the doctor came in—without Max. "I'm sorry," he said. "There was nothing we could do."

I went home in a daze. I felt so lost. But it wasn't really the fact that Max was gone that was upsetting me. It was the sudden, certain realization that things were totally out of my control.

Here was a being who had loved me and depended on me – a being who I had promised to take care of – but when the crucial moment actually came and he really needed me, I was powerless to help him. Powerless.

Tibetans describe this life as filled with three different kinds of pain. The first one is easy, for it is what we normally think of as pain— anything from a headache to a broken heart. It can be either physical or mental.

The second kind of pain is interesting, for it is what we would normally call pleasure. A delicious meal, a good job, a nice partner— all these fall into the category of something that brings us pain. Why? Because they will all eventually come to an end. Somewhere deep down we know this. So even as we seem to be enjoying the "pleasant" things that life brings us, somewhere there is this terrible awareness that we can't ever hold onto the things we enjoy, no matter how hard we try. Either the dinner runs out, or it just stops tasting as good. That is the way it goes with every single pleasure of life. We are never satisfied. And that is painful.

But the third kind of pain is the worst of all. It is called all-encompassing pain, and it is the one I caught a glimpse of after Max died: the simple fact that we have absolutely no control of what will come to us.

The Tibetans have a saying:

> In the end
> This life of pain
> Always reveals its true nature;
> But it shows itself
> To the fortunate long before.

We can live for a while in denial, pretend that everything is fine, but sooner or later you will be forced to look this life in the face. There *is* no one to turn to. We are helpless. Sooner or later the doctor will come to *you* and say, "I'm sorry. There's nothing we can do." And then where do you go for help? There is no one to turn to. We all know this deep inside, and it terrifies us.

Perhaps the best way to describe the third kind of pain is simply "your deepest, darkest fears."

It doesn't have to be this way. There is a place you can reach, a place beyond any of these three kinds of pain, a place of peace, a place of bliss.

Let's meditate, and envision it together.

6

The Nuts and Bolts

Here begins our first meditation. But we haven't yet talked about *how* to meditate, have we? The Tibetans have some strong views about how to teach meditation. The natural logical progression might be to begin with the technique, the "how to" side of things, and then once we've gotten that down, to move on to what to meditate upon. But in Tibet, they do them both at once. And there's a special reason for this. Tibetans insist that you should never practice meditation unless you are meditating on a virtuous object—something that will change your mind for the better. So even at stage one, we will have a nice, solid object of meditation.

In the old days, and perhaps now as well, there were people who became so wrapped up in the process of meditation that they lost the whole purpose for it. They spent their entire lives reaching deeper and deeper levels of watching their breath, and in the end got old and died like everybody else.

Meditation is just a tool. Like any other kind of tool, it can be used for good or for bad. Don't ever get caught in the trap of thinking that the meditation itself is the goal. It is just the road that gets us there, if we know how to travel it properly.

So we will begin like the Tibetans—learning technique and subject matter at the same time. Weaved in alongside the actual meditations will be these little sections about meditation technique, called "meditation tips," that will guide you in the more practical, how-to aspects of learning to meditate. Here's the first.

MEDITATION TIP

YOUR MEDITATION SEAT

You might think there is not much to say about simply sitting down on a cushion, but finding the right seat is essential for your meditation practice. Since the mind and body are integrally connected, the way you position your body will affect the way your mind works.

As meditators, we are looking for a seat which is so comfortable that we can leave our body behind entirely and enter into the world of pure thought. But at the same time, this posture needs to be one that helps stimulate our meditative concentration. It's no good to be comfortable if you are also slouching and half-asleep. And lastly, we need a posture that's stable enough to maintain itself—when our mind goes deep into its object, we don't want half of our focus watching our body to make sure it doesn't slump over.

The Tibetans have developed several very conducive meditation postures that fit these three requirements. Why several? Because every body is different. You need to try them out and decide which one is best for you.

We'll start from the bottom and work up—what do we sit on? Traditionally, you would first place a square of some kind of soft material down, about 3'x3' is big enough. It can be a folded rug or blanket, and it doesn't have to be very thick, just thick enough that your knees are not digging into the floor. Next you'd want to place another cushion under just your bottom, so that your seat is raised up a bit higher than your knees. Exactly how high is up to you, but it is important to try out different sizes and shapes of cushions to get the one that truly fits your body. (For instance, I know someone who swears by a small block of wood as the best cushion ever!)

One thing the Tibetans always say—make sure both top and bottom cushions are made of natural fabric, and not synthetic. These days, all sorts of meditation cushions are available on the web. I personally like the half-moon shaped cushions that are filled with barley husks—the barley is removable, so it is easy to adjust your cushion to the perfect height.

Next—how to position the legs? The most common position in Tibet is the half-lotus, where you sit cross-legged with one foot on the opposite thigh. Normally it is the left foot that goes up, and then the right is tucked underneath next to the groin, but I have known Lamas who do it the opposite way, so try both and see which is more comfortable for you.

You may choose to take just a simple cross-legged position, but placing one foot up on the thigh gives you a more stable foundation, which helps you keep your back straight. And keeping the back straight is crucial for good concentration.

Crossing the legs in full lotus position, with both feet on the opposite thighs, is another option. This pose is very powerful: it locks the body tightly in meditation position, and it works on the channels of the subtle body to give greater concentration. But if you are not very flexible, you can hurt your knees. If you want to try this I suggest you build up to it—sit in lotus for one minute per day, then when that becomes comfortable try five minutes, and so on.

Knees hurting you? As I said above, it is important to be comfortable. So if you are one of those people who can't sit in any cross-legged position without pain, then sitting in a chair is a better option for you. In that case, sit with both feet pressed firmly to the floor and, if you can, try and sit on the edge of the chair, keeping your back very straight without leaning against the back of the chair.

Next is your torso—the fine art of straightening and elongating your backbone. There is a balance we must find between leaning too far back and leaning too far forward. The first will make your mind wander, and the second will make you sleepy. So it is important that the spine is resting just so on top of the legs. First, the two bones known as "sit bones" on either side of your buttocks should be pressed firmly down into the floor (or chair), allowing your torso to stretch to the sky.

Then make sure all the vertebrae of your back are lined up perfectly—the ancient texts say like a stack of coins. To do so, you can imagine a string at the tip of your head tying each vertebra together; then picture someone above you pulling the string straight up, stretching out the space between each vertebra and lengthening your spine.

Lastly, gently pull your lower abdomen slightly in and up. When you reach a perfect state of balance, the posture will become effortless.

Now where do we put our hands? The first traditional position is what the Tibetans call "meditation hands." This is where you place your left hand down in your lap, palm up, with the right hand on top of it, and then touch your two thumbs together to make a steeple.

Technically, your thumbs are supposed to meet exactly at the level of your belly button, but if you are not sitting in the full lotus position they probably won't. And keeping the hands too low may mean you are leaning too far forward. So some meditators place a small cloth under their hands to raise the hands up to the right place.

The other classic position for the hands is to place them on our knees, with the thumb and forefinger joined together to make an O shape. The palms can either face up or down, whichever is more comfortable.

Relax the shoulders and pull them slightly back, expanding the chest area. The head should be kept level, with the chin parallel to the floor. Just as with the position of the torso, if the head is raised up, your mind tends to wander, and if it is dropping towards your chest, you'll tend to get sleepy.

Consciously relax your jaw—many people hold tension there without being aware of it. Your tongue can be placed gently against the upper palate.

Your eyes can be softly closed, or if that makes you sleepy they can be slightly cracked open. If you choose the latter, they should be looking down and unfocused.

There's a trick to learning how to unfocus the eyes; here's how to practice: bring one hand up close to your face, just beyond the tip of the nose. Focus your eyes on the palm of your hand. Now, keeping your eyes focused there, take away your hand. It takes some practice; but once you get it, this is quite comfortable.

Now you're ready to meditate!

MEDITATION

Pain and the End of Pain

◇ Get into a comfortable position, and fix your body still. Let your eyes fall closed, and focus on your breath for a few moments, to get the mind settled.

◇ Now, go over the first kind of pain in your mind: obvious pain. Think about all the times you've experienced this kind of pain, both mental and physical.

◇ Ask yourself a child's question: why must I feel these pains?

◇ Next, contemplate the second kind of pain: inevitable pain. Think of all the good things you have now in this life. Ask yourself—can I hold onto any of them? What will it feel like when these things are torn away from me?

◇ Now go even deeper, and ask yourself this question: will anything I ever get in this life really make me happy? Try to get in touch with our human tendency to be constantly dissatisfied with what we get.

◇ Then think about the third kind of pain: ever-present pain—that terrifying feeling of having no control, and no one to turn to for help.

◇ Do you know what pain will come to you next? Do you have any power to stop it when it comes? Let yourself feel a bit of that deep down fear below the surface.

◇ Now, imagine yourself without these three pains. Your body is no longer made of a substance that could be harmed. It is no longer flesh and blood, but pure light, adamantine and indestructible—a body that feels nothing but exquisite bliss. Stop and picture this for a moment—feel that you have this perfect immaculate body, the most beautiful thing you can imagine.

◇ Then imagine a mind free of every care or worry—a mind filled with peace, and love for every being. A mind that can reach out to the very ends of space, and know every existing thing in the universe. A mind that looks into all these things, and sees their true nature.

◇ Next, picture the power you have as this being, power to help all the people you love. You can emanate in any form at all, and go to them and teach them to become like you. See yourself now, sending out different forms, in all different directions of space.

◇ This is your future self—an Angel's body, an Angel's mind. It is your ultimate evolution, it is what you are destined to become.

◇ Stay here, still and quiet for a few minutes, and simply be the Angel.

◇ In closing, make a promise to yourself to get out of pain and reach the Angel's state of bliss.

7

If I Die Today

"You are so incredibly lazy! I can't believe how lazy you are."

"But holy Lama, I'm trying as hard as I can."

Sigh.

"You are in the back seat of a car. It is driving on a small road on top of a very high cliff. There is no driver, and the doors are locked from the outside. You are headed off the cliff to your fiery death. But you and your friend in the back seat are oblivious—you are playing card games and laughing.

"So answer me one question—is it fun?"

"Pardon?"

"Are you and your friend having fun, in the back seat of the car?"

"I guess, for the moment."

"And what would happen if you ever looked up and saw what was coming?"

"That moment would end very quickly."

"So, is it better to delay the looking up, so that you could have a few more seconds of fun?"

"No, it would be better to look up as soon as you could, because then you'd have more time to do something about it."

"Aha! You said it, not me. The moment ends here. It's time to wake up and get to work."

* * * * * *

Tibetans say we should do our meditation practice "as if our hair was on fire." We should have the same urgency to get out of this pain-filled place as someone who has just woken up in a burning, smoke-filled house. But it's hard—all the distractions of this life keep stealing away our time and our mind.

We keep telling ourselves, "I'll meditate later."

Then one day you look up and realize life has passed you by, the time is gone, and it is too late.

What would you do if you found out you had only a month to live? Would you start to live your life any differently? What if you had only a week? Or a day? What would you do with that day?

We live our lives thinking we have so much time left to do the things we dream of. But the truth is, we have no idea how much time we have. How many breaths are left in this body of ours? Enough to get us through another night? We can't say for sure whether we will even see the sun rise tomorrow.

Logically, if someone comes to you and tells you you're going to die, you say, "Yeah, I know, eventually." In our minds death is always much later down the road, something that happens to other people, something we don't have to worry about right now. So we live our lives in denial—in our hearts we don't really believe we are going to die soon. And it will be soon—it is always too soon. There are always things left undone.

This life, it is so short. It goes by in an instant. Tibetans say it is like a bubble on the surface of the ocean. You don't have time to waste, every moment is precious.

That is why Tibetans do a meditation to remind themselves that they could die at any time. It is not meant to be morbid—quite the opposite. It is meant to spur us on to do the things in this life that we really long to do, while we still have the time. We are living now, our bodies and minds are still functioning—Seize the Day! For who knows where we'll be tomorrow.

There is a special fear that comes at the moment of death—you feel a pain like nothing you've ever experienced at the center of your heart, and it feels as if the very essence of you is being destroyed, imploding, collapsing into the center. It is completely beyond your control, and it is terrifying.

We are so very attached to this body. Just imagine if you lost a single part—say, your eyes—how terrible that would be, how much you would miss them. Or if you lost the use of your arms and legs. Death is much, much worse. Everything is ripped away, all at once, as you futilely try to hang onto all it is that you call "me."

People tend to be blasé about their own impending death, especially younger people, because they are not really thinking about it. They tell me "I'm not scared of death." Ask someone with a terminal illness and they will show you a very different perspective.

That is the reason no one likes to go to cancer wards or hospitals or rest homes—because we are in denial of our own death, and it is unnerving to be reminded.

And that is exactly why Tibetan yogis of the past used to meditate in cremation grounds, sometimes sitting right on top of a rotting corpse—so they never forgot where they were headed if they didn't practice hard enough.

So, go ahead, be like the yogis—take a moment to look death in the face, and see what it is like to live life as if each and every moment was precious. You might come to find that there are a few things in your life you need to change. People have launched themselves into whole new careers after doing this meditation for a few weeks, because they finally realized that now is the time to do the things they always dreamed of.

If you really do this meditation seriously, you'll start to realize that the most important thing to do with our time is to devote ourselves to figuring out just how to get beyond this no-win situation—how to start to take control, and evolve into a being who no longer has to die at all..

MEDITATION

Walking Into Death

◇ Get into a comfortable seated position, and focus for a moment on your breath, watching the air as it passes out and then into your body.

◇ Picture yourself walking along a road. Along each side are houses. You walk by them until you are inexplicably drawn to one of the houses, where you turn off the road and walk up the path to the door.

◇ You enter the house, and find yourself in a big living room. The walls are covered with portraits of people you have know who have died. You stop to look for a moment into the eyes of each face, remembering.

◇ In the middle of the room is a big pile of bones, with a human skull on the top, staring at you. It is a portent of your own future.

◇ Stop now and feel the bones beneath your skin. Think of the flesh now covering them—even now it is already in the process of rotting away, getting older by the minute. Picture how it will be in the future—see your flesh fall off and return to the earth, leaving only the pristine white of this pile of bones behind.

◇ There is a door at the back of the room, and you walk through it to another, smaller room.

◇ In the middle of this room is a glass case. Inside the glass case is a large hourglass, and 2/3 of the sand has already poured into the bottom half.

◇ You realize that each grain of sand still in the upper half of the glass is the amount of breaths you have left in this body, before you die.

◇ You think to yourself: "If I could only turn back the clock, if I could only stop this speeding train I'm on that's rushing towards my death." You try to break the glass case to get to the hourglass, but it is no use—the case is made of sheer diamond.

◇ You realize then that there is no way to stop this inexorable process; death is coming, and there's nothing you can do about it. Focus on this for a moment, until you get a slight feeling of fear inside.

◇ Sitting next to the glass case is a stand, with a wooden box on top. Inside the box is a slip of paper, and on it is written the day of your death.

◇ You try to open the box to find out when you will die, but the box is locked.

◇ Think now for a moment what this means: you have no idea when you will die, you could die at any moment.

◇ Think of the plans you have in mind for your future: tomorrow, next week, next year. None of them are certain. You have no idea how much time you have left.

◇ Will you wake up tomorrow? You don't know. Try to feel the distinct possibility that you may not see another day.

◇ If you do wake up, what will you do with the time? Start to grasp how each and every moment in this life is precious.

◇ There is a door at the back of this room, and you walk through it into a hallway with glass walls.

◇ In the middle of this hallway is a concrete slab. You go and lie down on it.

◇ This is the moment of your death. Everything is fading away.

◇ Where can you turn for help?

◇ Behind the glass wall to your left are all the things you spent time to accumulate in this life— possessions like a car or house; money; position, authority, recognition. And you look at them and realize that all of them are absolutely worthless, for none of them can help you.

◇ Think about how much time in your life you have spent to collect these things—time you can never retrieve.

◇ Then behind the glass wall to your right are all your friends and family, your loved ones. They have their hands pressed up against the glass, but they can't reach you—they can't help you at this moment either.

◇ There is a table to the right of your death bed, and on it is a book, entitled: How to Stop Death. But you have lost the use of your limbs, and you can't pick it up; your eyesight is fading, and you can no longer read. Your mind too is fading—you can no longer meditate. It is too late—you waited too long, and now there's no more time.

◇ Come back now to the present moment, of yourself, still alive, still able to meditate. Rejoice in this precious time, this precious opportunity.

◇ Then, before you end the meditation, think about the day ahead and make a pledge to use your time today as if it were the last day you had left.

MEDITATION TIP

THE THREE TYPES OF MEDITATION

The first meditation we did, the one about pain, was called an "analytical meditation." There are three general types of meditation. In this kind of meditation, you usually take a point that you've been taught which you are not quite convinced about, and then you sit and work it out logically in your own mind, until you come to a satisfactory conclusion.

Analytical meditations take a bit of practice. At the beginning, sometimes we just don't know where to begin. There is one trick to doing them, and that is to do them in the "debate style." In the monastery the monks spend hours and hours debating with each other in the evenings. They sit under the stars and argue the finer points of Buddhist philosophy, sometimes until the wee hours of the morning, getting ever closer to Truth. There are no winners and no losers, only whatever understanding is gained by everyone by the end of the night. (Nonetheless, those arguments can sometimes get quite heated!)

Debate-style meditation is similar. You take a particular position in your own mind, like: "Life is pain." Then you create a devil's advocate—an opponent in your own head who says, "Come on! Life is great!" And you simply let them argue it out with each other until you reach a conclusion.

Sure, it's a bit like playing chess with yourself, it's a bit schizophrenic, but if you have doubts about something, those two opposing viewpoints are already there inside your mind. And you can't move on until this inner conflict is solved. So best to let them hash it out and get it over with.

In Buddhism, it's okay to have doubts about something, until you have proved it logically to be true. In fact, this kind of rational way of thinking is encouraged. This is not a philosophy where someone would ever say: "Life is pain, because I said so!" You must come to the understanding yourself, or else it is not a true understanding. So, analytical meditations are invaluable.

The second meditation we did, the one about death, is called a "review meditation." Review meditations are step-by-step progressions: you are moving systematically from one logical conclusion to the next. Or they could be visual: you move step-by-step from one image to the next, like a picture book. The meditation we just tried had both of these components.

In a review meditation, you are not in doubt about the subject. We know we are going to die. And we know we need to use our precious time. The point of these meditations is to carve these thoughts or pictures into our mind indelibly, so that throughout our day they are always there with us, in the back of our mind, helping us.

The third type of meditation, which we practiced briefly near the end of our first meditation when we held the vision of ourselves as the Angel, is called "fixed meditation." This is where you place your mind on one single idea or image, and hold it there, fixed, for a certain length of time. Fixed meditation is used to reach a deeper understanding, a deeper clarity, than one we can achieve with our normal discursive mind. We use the first two types of meditation to bring our mind to a certain place, and then when we reach that place, we stop and hold our mind, still and silent, on the object. We will talk more about this in the chapters to come.

8

How this World Really Works

These problems we've been talking about are not so simple. I mean, hunger and poverty are one thing—we can imagine how it might be possible to one day eliminate them. But the fact that we must get old and die and lose everything—this seems an inherent part of being a human. So right about now you should be asking me: how is learning to meditate going to change that? Are you going to teach us how not to die? That's a pretty big claim.

Well actually, yes, I am. It all has to do with how this world really works.

There is one simple word, one principle in Buddhism, which explains everything, and that is the concept of emptiness.

Emptiness.

It's easy enough to say, but in the monastery it takes the monks 25 years to get a grasp of what it means.

The basic idea is this: everything around you—all the people and things you see and hear and feel and interact with in any way—is not what it seems to be. The entire world that you have so much faith in is fooling you. Tibetans like to say it is like an illusion or a dream. It is empty of coming from its own side, it is empty of having any nature of its own.

Fire has no nature of being hot, no quality of being able to burn, within itself. And that's why some yogis can stick their hand in flames and not get burned. Water has no nature of fluidity and that's why some people can walk on it. So where is the heat, the fluidity, coming from? It is coming from you.

Everything you see, feel, hear, taste, smell, or even think of is a projection. It is all coming from your mind—a tiny picture, a mental image, that is projected from you and appears to you as something separate, something outside yourself. But it is not separate at all—it has everything to do with you. You are creating it.

Think of a small child who is watching a movie. They might think that the things on the screen were actually out there, that the big elephant they see on the screen was actually charging towards them. What the child doesn't understand is that all these images they are experiencing are just projections, coming from a little box in the back of the room.

It is the same for us. We are like that child—looking at the world, believing it is out there, when in actuality we are the ones projecting it.

Our projections are much more sophisticated—in addition to sight and sound, they encompass feeling and smell and taste as well. So nowadays we could equate them to a virtual reality game. And that's why they are so hard to detect. How could we ever catch ourselves, when we are so caught up in the game?

That's where meditation comes in. We can learn to shut off our senses for a few moments, and really analyze the true nature of our reality. Watch ourselves projecting our world from a tiny box inside our heart.

What good will that do? I mean, what is the point of knowing something is not "real" if it looks real and feels real and can affect me? It is different than a movie, because if I see the elephant come and trample me, and he breaks my legs, it hurts, regardless of whether or not I know it's a projection.

The important question is, can meditation stop the pain?

Yes.

The more we understand it, the more we will understand what causes the projections we experience. Why did the elephant come, and why did he trample you? Because if we figure that out—if we figure out the actual cause of the things that bring us pain—then we can rid ourselves of them forever.

So we need to get to a state beyond the projections, yes, but that is just the first step. Our goal is not to sit forever in some void. No, once we realize firsthand that our entire reality is in fact projected from our mind, we can use this knowledge to control the projections. Then we can simply reach inside that little box and re-write the script of our life, so there are no more elephants (or maybe only friendly ones). And once we master that, the sky's the limit: write the world of your dreams.

II.

Nyingje:
Opening Our Hearts

9

The Big Secret

Picture for a minute that you are on a bridge overlooking a busy freeway in Los Angeles. It is dark, and the cars are making a line of red and white lights that stretches for miles. Look down for a moment and watch the cars go by. Where are they all going? They are all driving around looking for the same thing.

Everyone around us is searching: searching for a way to make this life meaningful, searching for a way to be happy. Every single move we ever make is done for this one goal. But *nothing we ever do to try and make ourselves happy ever brings us happiness.* We try so many things—meeting the right person, landing the right job—but none of them seem to work. Hasn't anyone figured it out yet?

When I was younger, I went around the world in my search. I was desperate to find the answer. I climbed sacred mountains in India, I dove to the bottom of the ocean in Australia, I even went hang gliding. I had deep and meaningful relationships with people. I got blessed by Gurus. I started a "career." I must have experienced more in a few years than most people do in their whole life. But still I came out empty-handed. What's the secret?

If you go deep into meditation, if you look deep enough inside your heart, you will find the answer, just as the Tibetans have done.

The big secret to being happy is very simple—it is what all the world's religions have been telling us from the beginning.

If you want to be happy yourself, learn to live your life for others. If you want to be fulfilled, devote yourself to making other people happy. This is the one and only way to happiness.

It is obvious really, just a basic law of cause and effect. But we have been taught the opposite in our society for so long, that this very simple principle becomes hard to wrap our minds around. Instead, we've become habituated to fending for ourselves, competing when we have to, and otherwise not concerning ourselves with "them." When I lived in New York City, the rule was: if there is an unconscious man lying on the street, it is none of my business—just walk right by.

And that is why we live in a society filled with people who have anxiety and constant worry and depression and ulcers and low self-esteem. All of these problems could be eliminated by the simple act of getting out of our own little melodrama and turning our focus towards somebody else.

Why do we walk by the unconscious man on the street? It is not because we are bad people. It is not because we don't care. Mostly we have taught ourselves to block out other people's pain because we feel helpless to stop it, because we fear that if we let ourselves feel all the pain we see around us, it would be unbearable.

And it would be, if there was no way to help them. But there is a way for you to help them. In fact, you are the *only* one who can help them.

> *You will help everyone.*
> *You will take away the pain*
> *of every single man, woman, and child.*
> *You will save them all.*

How is this possible? Because of emptiness.

Think about how we described the world—it is really all a projection coming from your own mind, remember? If it's your projection, then you are the only one who can fix it!

Somewhere deep inside, we know this. We know the solution lies within us. And that is why our hearts cannot be at rest when we know there is still pain in the world and we are not doing all we can to stop it.

I'll tell you another story. We were about six months into our three-year retreat, and I was getting a little bit lonely. It is hard to withdraw from the world after being immersed in it your whole life! The only other living souls around me were non-humans—lizards, ants, rabbits, blue jays, coyotes, and cows—so I took to trying to befriend them all. It became a habit to feed everyone (except the lizards, who only ate live flies) my leftover breakfast toast and the like.

One cow in particular was quite fond of this little ritual, and would come around to the crack in my fence every day at exactly the same time to get her lunch. Now you may be wondering why it was that cows were wandering in the middle of an empty desert. Actually they were the property of a certain rancher named George, who let them wander all over and graze.

My cow friend didn't come around for a while, and then when she came back, she had a little baby boy calf. He was very cute, and kind of feisty, trying to chew on everything in sight like babies do. Then I noticed he had this plastic red tag shaped like a stop sign pinned through his ear, with something written on it. I looked closer. The tag said one word: "terminate."

It is the way it works in this country—girl cows are kept for milking, and boy cows are sold for meat. But it broke my heart to see this tag and at the same time to see his mom, my friend, next to him so proud, not knowing what was to come.

Then one inevitable day, my cow friend came back alone. And she didn't want any leftover toast. Her child was gone, stolen from her. She came to our fence, and just started banging her head against it over and over. She wouldn't stop.

What could I do?

Everyone is in pain, everyone needs our help. But it seems so overwhelming, where do we even begin? I mean, I don't have enough money to go and buy all the baby cows from all the ranchers in the US. It seems an impossible task for just one single person.

And it would be, if the world were out there the way we always thought it was. But it's not out there, it's in here, within you. And that makes everything completely possible to change. It's like a pebble dropped into a pond—taking one simple small action in my own personal life, like deciding I can do without eating meat or wearing leather, will ripple out and affect the entire world.

We can even change the world by just sitting down in one place, closing our eyes, and working on fixing our own mind. Because *everything* we see in our outer world is simply an echo of what's inside.

So go ahead, open your heart and think about the pain you've seen, not just in your own life but in the entire world. Think about who you'd like to help, what you'd like to change. Then think: I can change the world, I can stop pain, because this world I'm seeing is empty.

Now you're ready to start the meditation.

MEDITATION TIP

WHERE TO MEDITATE

Where should you meditate? It is important to pick the right place. For instance, you wouldn't want to meditate on your bed, because you are used to going to sleep there, and so whenever you go there the mind automatically starts to get sleepy. And you don't want to meditate right next to your computer, because your mind will start wandering to the work you have to do or the emails you want to write. And for obvious reasons, meditating right next to the refrigerator wouldn't be so good either.

You need to create a place where, whenever you go there, the mind automatically wants to meditate. So find a quiet corner (or dedicate a whole room if you have the luxury), and designate it as your meditation spot.

Section your meditation space off from the rest of the house. You can use a curtain or one of those Japanese screens. Now make a rule that you will do nothing but meditate here. No books, no dogs, no kids, no laptops allowed!

Make the place beautiful, but simple. There shouldn't be a lot of clutter. Always keep your meditation space immaculate. (Actually, it really helps to keep your whole house clean—clean house, clean mind! But let's start with this little corner.)

Even books can be distracting for meditation. It is not good to have a lot of written words staring at you as you meditate, because your eyes want to open up and read them. So if there are books where you are meditating, you might want to cover them up with a cloth.

In Tibet, the direction you face is also something to consider. Traditionally, it is good to position yourself so that you are facing either to the east or to the west. This has to do with the rotation of the earth—if you get to a subtle enough state that you can actually feel the rotation, and you are facing either north or south, you may start to feel a little lopsided! But I don't think we have to worry about that just yet. For now, face whatever direction feels the most secluded, perhaps with your back to the rest of the house (and the world).

It is customary to place a small offering table in front of you, with a few precious things on it to remind you of your goal—photos of people you really admire and seek to emulate, a statue or drawing of an angel, whatever speaks to you personally. It is also a custom each day to place some kind of offering there for them. Flowers, candy, a glass of water—something simple, that can be placed out fresh each day.

In Tibet the custom is to set out eight tiny cups called offering bowls, filled with water. Each of them represents a different offering for the senses: water for drinking, water for washing, flowers, incense, light, perfume, food, and music.

The idea behind these particular offerings is—if a distinguished guest were to come to your house for a visit—then these eight things would be what you'd want to offer them. Imagine you lived in Tibet, and you found out the King was stopping by to see you. What would you prepare for him?

First you'd offer your guest something to drink after their long journey. Second, since they'd either be on foot or horseback, you'd offer them a place to wash their hands and feet, with some nice warm bathing water. Third, you'd present them with a beautiful bouquet of flowers to please the eye.

Fourth, you might light some sweet-smelling incense. Fifth, you'd brighten up the room with candlelight. Sixth, you'd offer to massage their feet with precious oils. Seventh, you'd cook them a scrumptious feast. And eighth, you would arrange for some beautiful after-dinner music to be played.

The cups are filled with simple water, but you imagine as you fill them that the water is actually these eight different offerings. Then in your mind you offer them to the person or angel on your altar.

Are you offering these things to a picture? Of course not, pictures can't hear music or eat dinner! You are sending these offerings to the real thing, using the power of your mind. And as you do, believe that they are really receiving your gifts.

Then at night before you go to bed, empty out the offering bowls and turn them upside down on the table. That way you are ready to go if the angel comes for you.

MEDITATION

The Practice of Giving and Taking

◇ Get into a comfortable position and then fix your body still. Let your eyes fall closed, and focus on your breath for a few moments, to get the mind settled.

◇ Call to mind someone you know who is in pain. It could be either a physical pain or a mental one.

◇ Go to them wherever they are right now, and sit facing them. Although you can see them perfectly, you are invisible to them, coming to them in secret.

◇ Look inside them and see their pain. This pain takes on a physical form, as a thick black cloud of poison writhing inside their body.

◇ You feel an incredible sense of sadness that they are experiencing this pain. Now decide that you must take it from them.

◊ We are going to use our breath to help them. So now, as you breathe in, picture this black cloud condensing into a tiny evil black ball at their heart.

◊ Then on each successive in-breath, pull this black ball out of them—it rises from their heart to their throat, and then up further, coming out their nostrils. Next pull it through the air, until the black ball is suspended just in front of your own nostrils, but not touching you.

◊ Look now into your own heart, and see a tiny diamond light. This is the light of wisdom, that can destroy all pain.

◊ Focus again on the black ball of pain just in front of you, and decide that you must destroy it completely— both for the sake of the person across from you, and for the sake of ridding this world of pain.

◊ Then on one quick in-breath, draw the black ball inside you and down to the diamond light. As soon as the light and the ball meet, there is a brilliant flash of light, and the ball is completely destroyed.

◊ The light gets brighter and brighter and fills your whole body, then starts to pour out from the pores of your skin, so that you are glowing with white light.

◇ Look again at the person across from you. Their pain has miraculously disappeared, and their face is now serene.

◇ Now, on rays of diamond light that shoot out from your heart, send them every good thing—anything they have ever wished for, and more.

◇ As each ray of light touches them, see them getting happier and happier, until they too are filled with radiant light.

◇ At first, it may be easiest to do this practice with someone you feel close to. But the next step is to try this same meditation using someone you don't really know that well. And after that, if you really want a challenge, try it on someone who you're not that fond of, or who you have some tension with—you're guaranteed to have some really amazing results.

Helpful Hints

◇ It is very common to feel a bit of fear when taking the black ball inside of you. That is actually a really good sign—it means you were really concentrated before, when you were imagining what the black ball was. Being willing to take it in is what makes this meditation so powerful. Just make sure that when you do take the ball in, you see it completely destroyed, gone without a trace.

◇ When you are doing the giving part, use your imagination! There are no limits in the realm of the mind. Create the perfect partner for them, or the perfect job. Give them back their youthful body. Give them wings to fly in the sky—anything at all.

10

In Sickness and At Death

This practice of giving and taking is one of the most powerful meditations you can do, because it combines a mental visualization with the physical component of the breath—a combination primarily used in the more advanced teachings, but at the same time something simple that we as beginners can start with right away.

For this reason, it is the meditation most often given to help people who have some kind of sickness. My Lama and I have given this meditation to people with cancer, and we have watched some of them progress from a terminal illness to a state of perfect health.

So if you know someone who is ill, you can teach them this meditation. In this case, it would be more powerful for them to picture taking away the pain of someone who has the same sickness as they themselves have. Then, whenever they feel the pain or fatigue of the sickness, either in meditation or out, they should have a thought that they are taking on this pain for others, and thereby destroying it, so that no one in the world has to feel it ever again.

This same thought can be used when someone is dying—as they die, they imagine taking on the pain of the entire world within themselves, and destroying it. It is a perfect antidote for that terrible fear that comes when you die, and it allows people to depart with their very last action in this life one of a powerful goodness.

This is why the Tibetans love the story of Jesus—when they hear about how he took on everyone's sins at the moment of his death, they say: "Oh, he was doing the Practice of Giving and Taking! He must have been a Buddha."

11
Seeds

There's one problem that should be coming up for you at this point. Now I have said that this meditation of giving and taking is a good method for you to stop all the pain of everyone in the world. So does it work simply by imagining it to be so? Can I cure my dad's bad back this way? Is it simply a matter of positive thinking?

We all know by now that just wishing for something doesn't make it happen. We learned that long ago—the day we wished for a new bike for Christmas and it never came. The world is not in our present, conscious control. That doesn't mean though that we aren't projecting it. The reason we can't control what is happening to us right now is because the script of our present reality is fixed—it's been written already. By whom? By you, of course, in the past.

So here comes the real question: *How did I write that script?*

Get this: not only is the mind a projector, it is a video recorder as well. Every single thing we ever experience is recorded—imprinted in the mind, embedded like a fingerprint in clay. All we ever see or hear or taste or smell or feel or think—everything makes an imprint, everything is stored away. The Tibetan texts say the mind is making 65 of these mental imprints every second. That's 3,900 imprints per minute, 234,000 per hour and 5,606,000 per day—now that's a lot of imprints! Lucky for us the mind has a limitless storage capacity. Our mind has literally billions and billions of these mental impressions.

This data is imprinted in the mind and it stays there dormant like a seed, until the time is ripe. Then the mental imprint starts to grow, and gets projected—as a tiny part of our outside world. So even as we are living, even as we are experiencing the world, we are writing the script for our future experience. It's a nice little system that puts us on an endless cycle of cause and effect. (This is one proof that the Tibetan texts use for past lives, actually. Because how could there ever be a first imprint? But that's another story—back to how these imprints work.)

Many of these billions of mental seeds are what we call "neutral" ones: a register of the color red, the round shape of a cup. We are not so concerned with these. What we are really interested in is the positive and negative imprints we are making. Why? Because those are the two kinds of imprints responsible for all the happiness and all the pain in the world.

What's a positive imprint? Anything that brings you a good result. And a negative imprint would of course be anything which brings you a bad result. So how do we plant positive imprints? Take care of others. Take care of others and your whole world will change for the better. And how to avoid planting negative imprints? Avoid hurting others. Avoid hurting others and you yourself will never have to feel pain again.

So you simply must take care of others—it's in your own interest!

Let's go back now to the original question: how does this meditation really work? Well, it's not as if you can really heal your dad's bad back by imagining that you are taking his pain away and destroying it. But by doing that meditation, by simply watching yourself imagining taking his pain, you plant very positive imprints in your mind. And when they ripen, they ripen into seeing a dad whose back problem went away. Because seeing your dad with a bad back is your projection, and that's the very reason you can make it go away.

I taught this meditation in Ireland, to a group of very new students. One lady told me she meditated on her daughter, because she and her daughter were estranged and hadn't spoken in eight years. And the next day she came up to me all excited and said that after eight years of silence, her daughter had called her that very morning. Now it doesn't *always* happen that fast, it depends on how intensely you concentrate as you do the meditation, but you can expect results to come to you in the very near future.

MEDITATION TIP

LIMITING SENSE INPUT

There is a saying about mental imprints in Tibet: "nothing is lost." This can be really reassuring. For instance, when you are trying to do something nice for someone and they don't appreciate it at the moment, you can take comfort in knowing that the imprints are planted in your mind, and you will see a good result.

But imagine this: every single thing you ever see or hear or taste or touch or smell is stored in your mind. Hour after hour, day after day—millions upon millions of imprints. And eventually, they all resurface.

I didn't fully understand the implications of this fact until I went into the three-year retreat. You would think that being alone in the desert, far far away from any other human activity, it would be quiet. Peaceful. Tranquil. I thought so too. Ah, but I didn't take into account these nasty little imprints.

After about six months, strange things started to rise to the surface of my thoughts. I would be meditating nicely, when all of a sudden a scene from a movie I had seen maybe ten years before would pop into my mind. And there it would be—as crystal clear as when I first saw it, larger than life. Because that's what happens when your concentration starts to improve—you can remember every vivid detail. Memories too—personal scenes from my life would play themselves back, in much the same way they say happens when you die. At times this was helpful, but more often than not it was simply distracting.

Needless to say, I am now more careful about exactly what I put into my mind. Not to say I don't go to see movies anymore—actually, I love movies. But I am more aware now about exactly what I expose my mind to.

Most of us spend our days constantly bombarded by outer stimuli. We are seeing images on film, on TV, in magazines, on billboards, on the web—these images are flooding our minds, giving us no chance to ever sit down and process what we've taken in. And do we really *enjoy* overstuffing ourselves?

All this over-stimulation really hinders the process of stilling our minds in meditation, because actually it is aggravating to the mind. How can we expect our mind to sit down and be still after we've been poking and prodding it for hours on end?

So what is over-stimulation? We've already mentioned too much visual input. Watch how much time you spend on the internet. Cut down on TV. Too much auditory input is just as bad. Watch being surrounded by constant noise, from the radio or even just too much talking. Learn to sit with the people you love for a few minutes in comfortable silence, without always feeling like you have to fill up the gaps.

You should also try to avoid needing to chew on something all the time. We tend to have pretty bad eating habits in the West—we eat food for all sorts of weird reasons like when we are nervous or depressed, instead of just eating when we are hungry. And too much sexual activity is also not too good for meditation, mainly because it drains your creative energy.

What exactly is "too much" of anything? This is something you have to decide for yourself. All of these are perhaps difficult habits to break; the easiest way to change them is first by simply *noticing* what you are doing. Don't even try to stop it, just observe yourself. The process of observation itself will give you the impetus you need to change.

I am not saying you shouldn't enjoy yourself. On the contrary! The first song I listened to after retreat was the most breathtakingly beautiful thing I'd ever heard, because I had finally learned to really listen.

Go ahead, have a delicious dinner, or listen to a beautiful song. But don't half-listen to a song as you talk on the phone and check your email all at the same time. Sit down and close your eyes and give it your full attention—let the song take you away, let yourself truly enjoy it. For we are trying to make our outer world more like the inner one—striving to get a meditative concentration in every activity that we undertake.

12

The Line Between Us

In the end, we will learn how to completely put aside our own wants and focus on the needs of others. And we will understand that doing so is taking care of ourselves, for this is the only way to be truly happy. As the famous Indian master Shantideva says:

> Every ounce of pain I see
> Comes from trying to serve myself,
> And any happiness I see
> Comes from serving others.

But often when we are in the process of learning to open our hearts and take care of others, the demon thoughts will come. Thoughts of resistance, almost a fear, of the idea of stretching ourselves out so far. You'll start to think: "But I don't have time for all this—I have to take care of me!" This is the point when we should take a look at who this "me" really is.

If you think about it, since every person in the world is coming from your own mind, they are all your creations—they are all your children, in a sense. Each one is an offspring of your mind, each one is a part of you. So there is no reason in the world why we shouldn't love and care for *all* these children of ours.

"Oh, it's too much...there are too many...I can't possibly..." Nonsense! It is only because you have the habit of thinking of them as separate from you that you think this. They don't have to be.

We can cultivate a new habit—a habit of thinking of the entire world as one large body. Think about it: we take care of our whole body, even though it has many parts. What if you got a splinter in your foot and your hand refused to help pull it out, because the hand was not the foot? Eventually you'll realize that failing to take care of other people is the same kind of twisted logic. It only hurts you.

But we are so used to caring only for ourselves—how to break this habit? The great master Shantideva came up with a good solution. He said, don't fight your ingrained habits—don't try to take care of others. Just relax and take care of yourself. With one small difference—broaden your idea of who that self is.

Where is the line between ourselves and others? Does the line end at the edge of our skin? Does "me" stop at what I can physically feel? If someone asked us this question, we might reply, "Of course." But if you truly lived by that definition, and you were only taking care of yourself, then you would never buy groceries. Because you don't actually feel the hunger of the person you are buying them for. Your mind is creating some imaginary self in the future who might be hungry. We can figure out the desires of others as easily as we can imagine the hunger of our future self. Easier, because that future self doesn't even exist yet, but the people around us are here now, right before our eyes.

In reality, the line we draw between ourselves and others is constantly shifting, depending on who or what is important to us at the moment. Think of a mother, whose only child has just fallen and scraped his knee. She feels the pain, and she runs to tend the knee as if it were her very own, for she has drawn a line around her son—she sees him as part of herself.

Can we be like our mothers, to everyone? It is not impossible to imagine extending the line of who "me" is to include other people. Like I said, who we think of as part of the circle of "me" is really just a habit—and knowing what we do now, that everyone is simply our projection, how could we not call them a part of "me"?

I had an experience during the three-year retreat that drove this point home for me. When we first started, we decided to place our yurts about 200 yards apart from each other. This was enough distance to have some privacy, but still close enough to feel we were all in it together. Very soon after we all settled in, a strange thing started to happen—we began to be able to sense the other people in retreat, without ever seeing or hearing them. If one retreatant couldn't sleep, we could feel her, and we all had trouble sleeping. This wasn't due to any miraculous powers we had all suddenly developed, it would have happened to anyone. We were just finally quiet enough to be able to listen. We would see each other over a break period once every three months and compare notes about it: "Were you up all night 2½ weeks ago? I *thought* so!" It became quite commonplace.

Then around the middle of the retreat, one of the retreatants had to break retreat because her father was dying. And the funny thing was, even though she left the area and flew to another part of the country, *we all still felt her*. It didn't matter how physically far away she was. We had drawn a line around us all, and she was inside it.

Perhaps something like this has happened to you with someone you are close to—you may be away on a trip and suddenly get this feeling that you need to call home; and when you do, you find that you were needed. What it proves to us is that we can feel things beyond

75

our own skin, we can stretch ourselves out to encompass others if we choose to. It sounds like some kind of miracle, but really it is just another proof that everyone "out there" is in fact coming from our own mind.

And because the world is your projection, because all the suffering out there is your suffering, and everyone out there is your child, you must learn how to open your heart and help them, for it is the only way that you yourself can ever be truly happy.

There is another, deeper reason why we should explore stretching out our line of "self." The more we experience the constantly fluctuating nature of our identity, the easier it will be to understand our own emptiness. For—just as the entire world is a projection, an image of the mind—our sense of who we are is also just another mental image. There is no fixed, solid you. And as you do this meditation, you'll begin to realize just how true this is. It's really all one big package—all these meditations on opening our heart are actually leading us straight to emptiness.

MEDITATION

Exploring the Line of Myself

◇ Get into a comfortable meditation position, then let your body relax and fall still.

◇ Watch your breath for a few moments, trying to keep the mind focused on one single point at the tip of your nose.   Watch the air as it moves out and then back in.

◇ Now think about how you normally define the line between yourself and everything else. What is you, and what is not you? Find the line that separates you from everything else.

◇ This body—is it a part of you? Normally we identify very strongly with our bodies as ourselves.

◇ Now think of where this body came from—all the way back to when the sperm and egg joined together at your conception.

77

◇ This body comes from the bodies of two other people. What part of that sperm from your father or egg from your mother belonged to you?

◇ Think of all that sustains the body—the food and water and air that nourish it, that transform and become part of the body. What about those substances is you?

◇ Now go back to watching your breath. Watch the air as it enters your nostrils—at what point does the air become part of you? Isn't it the same air once it enters the body?

◇ Think about it—you have the habit of seeing this body, which is composed of all sorts of outer things, as a part of your self. That line you've drawn around this body in your mind, and labeled "me," is completely artificial.

◇ Once we realize that the self we are used to thinking about is just an artificial idea in our own mind, then we can play with the possibility of changing it. Let's see if we can widen our circle of our "self."

◇ Pick one person, someone you are close to, and decide: "They are a part of me. I will take care of them exactly as I would care for myself."

◇ Imagine what it is that this other you wants, what it is they need. Try and figure out the hopes and dreams of this new you.

◇ Now think about how you can make each of them happen. Make a plan in your mind of how you will go about fulfilling all your new desires. Really believe that they are now your own.

Helpful Hints

At the beginning, this way of thinking will feel very forced. But like anything we practice, it gets easier and easier.

At first, you don't have to actually act out fulfilling this other you's desires after you get out of the meditation. Just *thinking* about doing it will have a powerful effect on your mind.

But eventually, the line actually will shift, and you'll really start to feel that this person is part of you. And then you'll really *want* to do all you can to make them—I mean yourself—happy.

MEDITATION TIP

WHEN TO MEDITATE

There are four classical times for meditation: at dawn, midday, dusk, and midnight. When you are in a deep retreat, you meditate at each of these four times. Dawn is when the mind is sharpest, and since no one else is awake yet, it is extremely quiet. There is also a subtle balance of energies in the body as the sun breaks the horizon. This is the most favored time for meditation in both India and Tibet.

At midday, the mind tends to be at its most analytical, so it can be good for certain types of meditation. At dusk, when the sun is setting, we again get that same subtle balance of energies, but the mind is now in a more elaborative and imaginative state—which is especially good for visual types of meditation. At midnight most people are usually just tired! But it is a time when the mind is least attached to the body, and the meditations can be very deep.

Eventually, you may want to experiment with all of these times of day. But in our normal day-to-day lives, the most important thing is to find a time, any time, in our busy schedule.

If you want to be a meditator, the first thing you need to do is set aside a time each day when you will do it. Most people find mornings to be the best time, because their minds are clearer, and they are not so tired from the day. It is important to get on a regular schedule, so try to meditate at the same time each day. Then your body and mind will become habituated to it. It is just like if you happen to eat lunch every day at 12 noon—at 11:50am you start to think about lunch, and at 11:58am your mouth starts to water. If you meditate at the same time every day, then your body and mind will want to do it at that time, and you'll be halfway there before you even sit down.

If you really want to learn this high art of meditation, then *make the commitment*. Promise you will try to do it every day, even if it is only for 10 minutes. That is good enough at the beginning. It does no good to meditate for an hour one day and then skip three days—that is not how we train the mind. Training the mind is similar to how great athletes like gymnasts or dancers train their body—they must practice every day in order to keep themselves at their peak.

For how long should you meditate? That depends on the individual person. You should meditate for as long as you can concentrate deeply. It does no good to sit there and zone out, it just creates bad habits. So if that really good concentration lasts for only a few minutes, then meditate well for those few minutes, and that is fine. But as you progress, your ability to meditate will increase, and so you should keep increasing the time accordingly. Set yourself a goal, try for instance to get up to an hour each day of deep, concentrated meditation time.

Give yourself the time. Meditation shouldn't be something that you squeeze into a spot of free time here and there. If you are really going to use it to save the world, then meditation is the most important thing you'll do each day. So pick the time when your mind is at its best and reserve it for your meditation; then schedule the rest of your day around that.

13

Ngagyel

Deep in our heart, we all want to be someone like the Dalai Lama, or Mother Theresa, or Mahatma Gandhi—someone whose immense love for others forces them to reach out and change the world. But how do we get there? It sometimes feels like we are miles away from that place. I mean, sometimes we can't even go through a day without getting annoyed/upset at _____ (fill in the blank!).

Anyone who has tried the advanced version of the practice of giving and taking will quickly come to realize that it is hard to imagine caring for someone who doesn't like you much. And almost everyone has a few people like that in their lives. But if we truly want to reach our goal, we have to learn to get beyond that: we must learn to love everyone, regardless of who they are or what they think of us.

This kind of equal status towards everyone is the Tibetan concept of equanimity. This word "equanimity" is very commonly used, and well-known as a Buddhist practice, but I'm afraid it has often been misrepresented. Equanimity doesn't mean that you should no longer care about people or have any kind of deep relationships with them. Equanimity isn't turning off all your emotions and feeling the same neutral way about family and friends as you do strangers in the street. Not at all.

Real equanimity is taking our deepest feelings of love for a particular person and then trying to feel that very same intensity for everyone else.

And wow! Imagine what that would feel like! Being in love with the whole world—your feet would never touch the ground.

Let's examine what is getting in the way of our true love for everyone—what are our obstacles?

When I was a young girl my parents used to send me to sleepaway camp for two weeks in the summer. It was fun for me, and I suppose a welcome break for my mom. When you first arrive at camp, the counselors assign you to a certain dorm room. There are usually about 8-10 girls to each room. Now at the beginning you don't know any of them, but you *know* that by the end of the two weeks about three of them will be your best friends, and then two or three will be people who you don't like, and then the rest will be neither one nor the other—sort of neutral. Tibetans say it's always like that. They say that to be human means to have a pretty equal mix of good and bad imprints, so whenever we walk into a room, no matter what room it is, it will be pretty evenly divided into thirds: who we like, who we dislike, and who we don't care about.

How does our mind go about deciding who is our friend and who is not? It is all a process of trying to establish our own identity.

Think for a minute about the people you like and those you don't like—the ones we choose to surround ourselves with and the ones we avoid. Most often, the main reason we like people and want to be close to them is because they think well of us, or they reflect a side of us that is pleasant and that we want to identify with. We use our friends and loved ones to define who we are.

This might sound a little cold-hearted, but if you think about it, it's true: why you want to love one person and not the other usually doesn't have anything to do with *them*—it has to do with what you perceive they are giving *you*. Every relationship we have is in some way imbued with this self-interest. And so it is tainted—it is not true love for the person.

Learning how to truly love means not having any selfish agenda. You'll know when you've reached this, because you will no longer discriminate between one person and the next—you will love every person equally.

Sometimes I like to fantasize about how my life could have been different: if I had turned right instead of left, if I had gone to that other college, if I had stayed in Nepal a few more months...I would have met a whole different group of people. Given different circumstances, anyone out there could be your best friend or lover or child or enemy. And who knows? Maybe in the future they will be. Everything changes. So choosing between people who will get your love and care and affection is silly.

They *all* need your love. They are all suffering. And whether they know it or not, they are all depending on you.

Ok. Say I've convinced you that it is logical to love everyone equally. Still we have a problem in trying to carry it out. These habits we have of relating to people—our *relationships*—get in the way. Even the good relationships we have with people can be limiting. A friend of mine was recently talking to me about his father, and how he couldn't really talk to his father seriously about any deep ideas because his father still thought of him as 12 years old. And my friend is nearing 50! We've all gone through this—anyone who's ever gone home to see the family for the holidays and gets thrown back into the same childhood roles knows what I'm talking about.

The people we love shouldn't limit us. It is not that we shouldn't have these relationships. We simply need a method of getting beyond who they think we are. We need to take control and create our own identity. A new, pure identity: one that does not rely on how other people see us. One that will allow us to be who we need to be in order to save them.

Tibetans call this *ngagyel*—developing a sense of divine pride. It is the sacred art of consciously creating who you really want to be, deep down inside. Deep down, all of us want to help others. All of us want to save the world. And so we plant the seeds to become that person, by imagining we are already there.

A very good way to work on this sense of divine pride is to work on the way you relate to everyone around you. You need not change anything at all in your outer world, but in your inner world, in your meditation, everything is different. There, everyone is like a small child that reaches out to you, who needs your help and guidance, who is waiting for you to show them the way.

And if you do this meditation, it will carry over to your outer world. You will start to develop a secret identity: underneath that Clark Kent exterior of this normal person going to work or fixing dinner or taking out the garbage is this secret awareness of who You really are, and who You are going to become.

Now think to yourself: I *will* be the one to come to all beings and touch them and take away their pain. You must practice thinking this so much that you start to believe it. Because it's true. You are the One.

MEDITATION

Child Meditation

◇   Close your eyes, and focus on your breath for a few
     moments. Watch the air as it goes out and then back
     into your nostrils. Try to keep your mind fixed there
     on that single point.

◇   Now call to mind someone whom you normally see as
     higher than you. It could be someone like a boss at
     work, or someone like your older brother, who does
     everything better than you. Picture them sitting just
     across from you, as we did before.

◇   Get out of the normal role you have with them, and
     try to look at them objectively. They are struggling to
     find happiness just like everyone else. They too are
     suffering. They too need help.

◇ Now think of your normal role with this person as just a disguise—in reality you have been sent to help them, to save them from all pain. See yourself now as the One who will do this.

◇ Imagine this person as they would have been like when they were a small child. That child is still there in their heart, needing your love, needing protection. Look inside their heart and see this child there. Reach out and take the child's hand, and promise them that you will help them.

◇ Now try this same meditation with someone who you feel has hurt you in the past, establishing this new identity with them. Practice it until there is no more hesitation about helping them.

MEDITATION TIP

ZOOMING OUT, ZOOMING IN

When we are in meditation, the possibilities become infinite, and we are no longer limited to living within the space of our bodies. We can become as big as a planet, or as small as an atom, whatever we like.

It is good to start to flex these mental muscles a little bit, for this technique will come in handy for many things. For instance, in the very most basic exercise of watching our breath, we can use it to get a sharper focus on our object. Instead of picturing ourselves in our body watching this tiny part of ourselves as it moves, we take ourselves in deeper, so our entire focus is just the tip of our nose. We zoom in,

just like the lens of a camera, so the nostrils are now these huge caverns, with powerful gusts of wind flowing out and in. Then maintaining the focus becomes easy.

◇   Just how far can we zoom in? Here's a little meditation exercise to find out.

◇   Imagine that at your heart is a tiny sphere of light, about the size of a mustard seed.

◇   Now zoom in, so that you can see it up close. It becomes to you as large as a room.

◇   There inside this white orb is an Angel.

◇   Zoom in again to see inside Her heart, and you will find She has a tiny white sphere there.

◇   Now zoom in further to check inside it, and you find another Angel.

You will come to the realization that you could keep going on like this forever, and never reach an end. It is the same when we zoom our minds out: we can encompass a whole city or country or planet or solar system or galaxy, as far as we wish to travel. The universe has no edges, and there are absolutely no boundaries to the mind.

III.

Karma:
Mental Imprints

14
Like Gravity

My Teacher pulled something out of his pocket. He held it up and asked, "What is this?"

"A pen," I said.

"Are you sure?"

"Yes."

Then he whistled loudly and called out, "Tsering." And the little dog came padding in, wagging his tail.

"Tsering, what is this?" said my Teacher, as he held the pen out for the dog to see.

And Tsering jumped up and grabbed it in his mouth, and went padding off to a corner to chew on his new toy. (He had it all day, and I checked—he didn't write with it once.)

That day I saw the emptiness of that pen—*I* may see the black stick thing as a pen, but the dog would disagree. The dog doesn't see a pen at all. To the dog it is a new toy—something to chew on.

And that is proof that the pen I think I see is not really out there, it is just an image in my mind—a tiny picture of "pen" that my mind is overlaying onto the black stick. How is this proof? Because if the pen was really out there like I thought it was, then everyone would have to see the same thing—everyone would see the same pen as me.

But no matter how long I held it up and tried to explain the idea "pen" to Tsering, he just wouldn't get it.

Tibetans would say that is precisely what makes him a dog and me a human being—I can see pens and he can't. I have mental imprints in my mind that project out as pens, where he has imprints that are projecting as chew toys.

Every single disagreement in the entire world can be traced back to this same story—two parties who have different imprints in their mind, and who therefore see things in two totally different ways. That's why there are different radio stations. That's why there are 31 ice cream flavors and not just one. Because raspberry sorbet is not self-existently the best flavor in the world. (In fact, I think I may be in the minority on that one.)

But this brings up an interesting question: why then do many people see the same thing? Why would all the other humans in the room also agree with me that there's a pen out there? We have similar mental images ripening in our mind because we all did similar things in the past—here, namely, we wrote things that helped other people learn something. Or maybe we just gave away lots of pens.

This explains things like the borders between countries. If you go and stand at the border, there is no physical line between Mexico and America. The land looks completely the same. But on one side many people are poor. And on the other side, people have more than they need. Where is the line—what divides these people? The people on one side all did something very generous together in the past. And so their mental imprints ripen as a group. In the ancient texts they call this "group karma."

So whether we are seeing something in the same way as someone else or differently, the important thing to realize here is that there are certain laws, certain correlations that dictate how our world appears. And in order to change our world, we must know *how* to change it— we must learn what impressions to plant in the mind in order to see the things we want appear. Tibetans call this the "law of karmic correlations."

You can think of it as an input/output scheme: what must I put *into* the mind in order to see such-and-such come *out* of it? What must I *stop* putting into the mind in order to stop seeing this other thing?

There is a very helpful chart that was compiled by an ancient Tibetan named Geshe Chekawa, which will start to help you understand these correlations. You can find it at the end of this chapter. It will give you enough of an understanding of how these things work to be able to work out the rest yourself.

But there is one very basic law to remember: every mental image that comes out was caused by something you did to others. If it is a pleasant image, it has been caused by something you did that helped others. If it is unpleasant, it is from something that hurt someone else. The cause is always similar to the result: if you want a new car, you'd want to help people get places; if you want better health, you'd want to take care of a sick person; and so on.

This next meditation is called, "Planting Seeds to Change your Life." When my Lama and I travel around the world to teach, this is the one thing we end up teaching the most. Why? Because if you do this practice sincerely, it produces quick results that you can actually see in your immediate life. And this gives people the incentive to continue in this path and practice even more.

This meditation is more than something you do when you sit down on your cushion—it is training you to think in a certain way, to hold a certain view of the world—the View that every single thing comes from your own karmic seeds. So practice it now, in the quiet of your meditation space, but then try to take it with you everywhere you go.

*

MEDITATION

Karma Meditation–
Planting Seeds to Change Your Life

◇ Get into a comfortable position, then hold your body there, still.

◇ Focus on your breath for a few moments, watching the air flow out and in.

◇ Now, think of something that you want in your life that you don't have now. It could be anything—a new job, or promotion, a girlfriend or boyfriend, more money.

◇ Think of all the usual ways people try and get the things they want—a good resume, a new diet, a surefire investment. Do they work? Sometimes, for some people. That means they are not the actual cause. Think of all the ways you've tried to get this thing that haven't worked for you in the past.

◇ Now reflect on why it hasn't worked; remind yourself of how everything is a projection, and how we have to create the right mental imprints in order to get the things we want.

◇ Think again about what you want to see projected in your life, and now figure out the real cause to get that thing: what imprints do I have to plant to see myself get it? This is pretty easy to figure out—it always has to do with helping others. If you want a nice job, help others find one. If you want a good partner, honor others' relationships. If you want more money, be generous to others.

◇ Imagine yourself doing what you need to get the thing you want.

◇ Then see the mind at work, recording what you have just done—watch yourself plant a mental imprint.

◇ Now look into the future, and imagine how it will be when you are forced to see yourself get what you want.

SOME EXAMPLES OF...

Problem	Karmic Fix
I don't have enough money	Be radically generous with your money, help, and time
I can't seem to hold onto a partner	Respect other people's relationships
I have some health problems	Take care of others who are sick
I don't get enough respect	Give power and responsibility to others
I'm looking for a companion	Befriend a lonely person
I'm depressed	Focus on someone else's problems
My plans and projects always seem to fall through	Keep your promises, however small

ACTUAL CAUSES AND RESULTS

Problem	Karmic Fix
I can't sleep at night	Send someone love
I don't have enough energy	Appreciate all that others do for you
I eat poorly	Make sure someone else has a good healthy diet
I don't feel attractive	Stop getting angry
I have too much stress and anxiety	Alleviate someone else's fears
My mind is too restless to meditate	Work to be kind to everyone you meet throughout the day
I don't understand emptiness	Share your ideas about emptiness with others

15
Why Things Die

We talked about how things in this life always end, always get old and die out on us. Everything from your favorite shirt to your relationship to your own body. But *why*? Why does everything have to go?

Tibetans say the birth of something is the herald of its death—the very fact that you were born means that you must someday die. The very fact that something like the place you live in was built means that it will someday come crumbling down.

This has to do with where all these things are coming from, how they came about. As we now know, they are all ripening from imprints that we planted in our mind, from something we did in the past.

Imprints work in much the same way as a seed that you plant in the ground does. There are certain rules that must be followed. For instance, the result is always similar to its cause. You don't plant rice seeds and expect to see barley pop out. And this particular rule is where all the clichés about karma come from: "You get what you give"; "It all come backs to you"; "What goes around comes around," etc.

Then there is that gestation period between when things are planted and when they ripen. You don't plant a rose seed and then sit there expecting roses to appear that same day. Things take time to grow. Tibetans say this time gap is really the source of all our problems. If, the moment we took a bite of a chicken leg, our own leg started to ache, there would be no more discussion about whether or not to eat meat!

There is another way that mental imprints are like seeds, and this is the reason why things die. Think of a seed turning into a sprout. What happens to the seed when the sprout starts to come out? It is destroyed—its power as a seed, as a *potential,* is finished. The result has occurred, which means that its causes can no longer exist.

The very ripening of a seed or a mental imprint means that the power of the seed is being used up. The flower—and its resultant experience in our outer world—has a certain fixed lifespan, a certain number of hours or days or years that it will exist, depending upon what kind of seed you planted.

For instance, we planted a certain number of seeds in order to see ourselves in our present body, in our present life. But they are all, one by one, being used up. Our karmic credit card is running out. That is why we see ourselves getting older. And that is why we have to die.

This is how seeds ripen in the normal course of things, where we are constantly planting imprints in our mind without having any awareness that we are doing so. Tibetans call that kind of mental imprint an *impure* karmic seed.

Why is it impure? Because eventually it wears out. But there is a way to plant pure karmic seeds in our mind—ones that won't wear out. All we have to do is be aware of what we're doing as we plant them.

How does that work? Won't the seed still disappear once it ripens? That is very true. But when we are aware of planting a certain mental image, that awareness plants another mental image right alongside of it—an imprint for wisdom, or you could say a habit to keep planting that seed.

Say, for instance, you are generous to a certain person—later on, the mental imprint you planted will ripen as something you want, like money, coming back to you. And you will enjoy that result, and in the process the karma will wear out. But now imagine that when you were generous to that person, you had a clear awareness in your mind that you were planting a mental imprint—one that would ripen as someone being generous to you.

Now when the result occurs and someone is generous to you, you would naturally want to take some of the money you received and give it to someone else. And this would create even more money coming to you, and you'd continue perpetuating this by continuing to give it away.

You would get into an upward spiral, creating bigger and bigger results, because as you understood more and more where the money was actually coming from, you'd naturally want to give more and more.

This is how we create our own perfect world—with a multitude of these upward spirals, due to the simple fact that we understand what we are doing.

16
Limitless Thoughts

Once you start experimenting with this in your own life, you start to realize pretty quickly that it has everything to do with intention. Tibetans say: "Simply *thinking* is karma in its raw form." And that is why we can change our world simply by sitting down in meditation. (Although there is a great power to following through with actual acts of kindness towards people; and we must learn to do both.)

Because things are empty, because they have no nature of their own, we can use the power of our intention to make every action we do meaningful. Even the simple act of giving a few crumbs to a bird can have profound effects, if you have the right thoughts while you're doing it. You need not go and make drastic changes in all the activities of your life in order to see some substantial results. You simply need to change your mind. Change how you think about all the things you normally do.

Tibetans call these limitless thoughts, because they ripple out later into our world as limitless results.

What are you normally thinking as you get dressed in the morning? What kind of intention do you have as you eat your breakfast? Most people would say, "Not much." But people never do anything without a reason. If you look closely, there is some vague thought about wanting to look nice, or wanting to feed yourself because you are hungry. Basically, it is all about you. We have this habit of thinking about ourselves about 23 ¾ hours of the day.

Tibetans have a practice where they turn this kind of thinking completely around, so it is all about others. "Why am I getting dressed this morning? So I can help every single living being reach their ultimate evolution into a Being of pure happiness."

"Why am I eating breakfast? I need to nourish this body, so it can continue to work for the sake of every person on this planet, and beyond." The action that we do may be just the same as before, but now it has a completely different intention—an intention that will dramatically change your world.

Every single small action in your life can be done for others. This is a meditation you can practice doing anywhere, at any moment of the day—driving your car, taking a shower, even watching TV! As my Lama always says, "Use the time."

It's fun to do secret acts of goodness all day long: acts that no one else is even aware of. Look around as you drive your car to work, at all the other people out there. Then, perfect your intention—see yourself driving to work in order to help them.

When you master this way of thinking—when you really *are* living your life for the sole purpose of helping everyone (including yourself) get enlightened—then they will call you a *bodhisattva*: a person who is headed straight for Enlightenment.

Now you are starting to see why it is so important to learn how to open our hearts to others. Because it is others that get us enlightened.

The practice is called "Four Limitless Thoughts of a Bodhisattva." Here's how we do the meditation.

MEDITATION

Limitless Meditation

◇ Get into a comfortable position, and let the body fall still.

◇ Take a couple moments to simply watch your breath, as it passes out and then back into your body.

◇ Now focus your mind on the people who live and work around you, the people you see every day.

◇ Think about how every day, each one of them is struggling to find happiness and avoid pain, just like you. We all want to be happy.

◇ Then observe how none of them is really finding this happiness; observe how much pain there is for them in this life.

◇ Let your heart open to them, and think to yourself: "I wish they could all find happiness. I wish they had no more pain."

◇ Now go one step further. Remember how they are all a projection, and how because of that fact, you have ultimate power to change them. Then take personal responsibility, by cultivating the following Limitless Thoughts:

◇ Think to yourself: "I will make sure everyone has every happiness they could ever wish for."

◇ Think to yourself: "I will take away all their pain."

◇ Think to yourself: "I will bring them to the highest happiness of enlightenment itself."

◇ You are ready for the final Limitless Thought. Think to yourself: "And I will do this for every single being, leaving no one out."

◇ Now broaden the scope of your focus so that it encompasses the entire world, and think: "Everyone is the same. They all want to be happy. I must help them."

◇ It's a very simple meditation, with very profound effects.

◇ What kinds of seeds are planted when we think limitless thoughts? We'd definitely be on an upward spiral. Not only are they seeds that perpetuate themselves, but these simple acts plant seeds that become the cause for your own enlightenment. Why? Because thinking that you want to help others get there is the exact powerful seed we need to plant to see ourselves get there. It is the same old karmic story.

◇ These kinds of thoughts are a karmic inferno that spreads out to the ends of the universe, like wildfire. Because now, every time you do something, you're doing it for your whole self—not just for that one tiny part you normally think of as you. So your whole self benefits.

◇ You could even go so far as to say that you don't ever plant a pure karmic seed until you are planting this kind of limitless seed. For it is this kind of upward spiral that makes it possible to change our world from something ordinary to a perfect paradise.

17

Four Powers

Whenever my Lama and I give a teaching about the laws of cause and effect, no matter where we are in the world, there is always a certain point when some new student in the room really starts to understand the implications of the karmic laws of cause and effect.

Sooner or later, this person will always raise their hand to ask us one burning question: "But if this stuff you say about mental imprints is true, then I have already planted billions of negative imprints in my mind—is there any way to get rid of them?"

Once you start to understand the nature of this world, and how it is all coming from things that you did to others in the past, you inevitably start to reflect on all the negative imprints you have unknowingly planted in the past. A wave of regret then washes over you, for you know that something unpleasant is surely headed your way. How do you avoid it?

Perhaps these seeds are already starting to ripen. Perhaps certain habitual problems you've always had begin to make a little more sense. Whether we remember doing the negative thing that caused it or not, the fact is that we *must* have done it at some point, for results cannot happen without a cause. The question is, how can we get rid of them?

All of us have certain obstacles in our life—certain things that keep getting in the way of what we want. It could be an outer obstacle, or even an inner tendency within ourselves that stands in our way. One Tibetan Lama I know called them "blockers," which is an apt name, because that's exactly what they do—they block us from reaching our desired goal.

There is a special meditation for getting rid of these karmic blockers. It is called the Four Powers.

In this meditation, we are going into the mind itself, to seek out and destroy negative imprints we have planted in the past, before they have a chance to ripen, before they can cause us any more pain.

MEDITATION

Four Powers Meditation

◇ Think of something negative that you've done, or else think of a negative result in your life that you are having trouble with.

◇ Example: I got upset at my partner today.

FIRST POWER: THE POWER OF TRUTH

◇ Bring up your clearest understanding of emptiness and of how the world really works—how everything is simply a projection of your own mind. Everything is the ripening of something you've done to others in the past.

◇ Now apply that to your present situation. Either reflect on the negative result that will occur because of your negative action, or figure out what negative action you must have done to cause your present negative result.

◇ Example: because I got upset at him, I will now be forced to see people upset at me in the future.

SECOND POWER: THE POWER OF REGRET

◇ Take a moment to truly regret doing that negative thing, knowing it will only cause you pain.

◇ Example: I really don't like it when people get upset at me. That was a really dumb thing for me to do, planting that seed.

THIRD POWER: THE POWER OF RESOLVE

◇ Decide that you are not going to do that thing again. If necessary, give yourself a certain time limit, something that you can actually do, then build up slowly to longer and longer time periods.

◇ Example: I am not going to get upset at my partner for the rest of the day.

FOURTH POWER: THE POWER OF ACTION

◇ Now make an action plan—decide what antidote activity you will do to clean up this negative imprint. Try to relate it to what you are purifying.

◇ Example: To make up for getting upset, I will cook his favorite dinner.

MEDITATION

A Fire Meditation

I have fond memories of the first time I learned the fire version of this four powers practice, on a beach in San Diego with my Lama. The sun had set and it was getting dark as we dug a hole in the sand, and then filled it with some old newspaper, a few sticks, and some small logs. I lit a piece of paper underneath, and then my Lama poured some clarified butter over it, and it burst into flame. Then he took out a pouch filled with tiny round yellow seeds and poured some into my hand.

"These seeds are your karmic obstacles," was all he said.

I stared at the seeds in my hand. I thought of all the demons inside of me—my laziness, my selfishness, my pride—and I pictured each of them, hiding there inside the seeds.

A fierceness welled up inside of me then—a holy battle cry. "I will destroy you!" I thought at them, and threw these demon seeds straight into the heart of the flames.

We sat there for a good half and hour, together in silence, taking small handfuls of seeds and throwing them into the fire. I would alternate between calling up my new wrathful persona, and going over the four powers step-by-step for each of my spiritual "blockers."

Whenever the seeds met the flame, there was this incredibly satisfying "Pop!" as it was incinerated. And I started to feel lighter and lighter as all the things weighing on my conscience were washed away.

Now my Lama and I do this practice every two weeks, as is the custom of monks in the monastery. I have grown to love the sweet smell of burnt mustard seeds.

Our practice has evolved over time; now, in addition to the seeds, we sit and write out a list of both the best and the worst things we have done during the last two weeks. Next we carefully cut the list so that each item is on its own separate slip of paper. Then as we sit before the fire, we take turns showing each other our little slips of paper before throwing them into the flames.

First we do all the negative items on our list, and we see the fire completely destroying them. (Then we usually have some popcorn and cocoa to celebrate.) After that, we do all the positive items on our list, taking a moment to rejoice in each one however small, and then we send them out through the smoke of the fire as an offering to the world. It is a beautiful practice, something you can do together with other people on a regular basis to help each other lighten your hearts.

Since we don't always have the luxury of a beach nearby, let me introduce you to the portable fire purification kit that we have developed in our travels. Here is what you will need:

- A tin can, something like the tins that loose tea is packaged in. It can be quite small, around the size of a grapefruit, or it can be larger, around the size of a watermelon
- Some old scrap paper
- A lighter or matches
- Several small sticks (your mini logs)

- Some clarified butter (or in a pinch some cooking oil will do)
- A tablespoon
- Paper and a pen
- Scissors
- A bottle of yellow mustard seeds

Write out your list of positive and negative actions and cut them carefully into strips so that each item is on its own separate slip of paper. Make one pile for the bad ones and another pile for the good. Crumple up some of the scrap paper and place it at the bottom of the tin. Then place a few of the small sticks on top of that. Pour about a tablespoonful of clarified butter on top, and then light some paper beneath. Now you're ready to begin the practice!

Once you have your kit together, you can do the fire practice anywhere at all. A few words of practical advice: the tin can get *quite hot*, so place it on something that will not burn, like cement or a ceramic plate. (We have scarred a few wooden tables this way.) Also, be careful of the fire alarms in hotel rooms. If possible, do it by an open window, *away* from the alarm, and make the fire very small, or you will have some explaining to do!

18

The Biggest Demon of Meditation

You can work on your meditation for weeks or even months, and be making some nice steady progress, but then a demon comes, and in one minute smashes all your hard work to dust, leaving you back at square one.

Who is this demon? Where does he come from? He is someone you are very familiar with, for he is living right inside your own heart—he is your anger.

Just a single moment of anger destroys thousands of positive mental imprints, leaving you in a darker, uglier world. It is the greatest enemy of meditation, for it is simply not possible to ever reach stillness when your anger demon is still running around rampant.

The Tibetans, they have sat in the snow for years meditating, they have lived only on nettles, they have put themselves in a tiny box and slept sitting up—they understand spiritual hardship! And they say that *the very hardest thing in the world to do* is to stop yourself from getting angry when someone has just pressed all the right buttons.

If you've ever tried this, to stop anger just as it is rising, it's like standing in front of a moving train and trying to stop it with your bare hands. It just runs you right over. So what to do? How to master this ultimate spiritual challenge?

There are many methods the Tibetans use to control the mind when it is about to get angry. The first is reflecting on how anger does you nothing but harm—it gives you ulcers; it keeps you awake at night; it makes you unpleasant to be around, so that you end up without any friends; and it destroys all the good imprints in your mind, so that your whole world starts to look darker.

This method is useful for avoiding that negative tendency to "hold a grudge", or dwell on how someone has hurt us.

Another method is a simple phrase:

> *If you can do something about it, then why get upset?*
> *If you can't do anything about it, then why bother getting upset?*

Basically this beautiful phrase is just reminding us that any time we get upset about *anything*, it is just a waste of time, and doesn't help matters at all.

It is especially useful for dealing with the small crises that come up in life—like when you are late to an important event, and then get stuck in traffic.

The texts then go on to describe how anger rises in the mind. Something happens that we don't expect, and first we

119

get a little off-balance. Then, when we decide it is unpleasant, we get upset. And that then leads to anger. So they say that you should try to watch your mind and catch it at the off-balance stage, while it is still fairly easy to stop the momentum.

Now all of this is very helpful advice on learning to control the mind, but at the crucial moment when you are just about to get angry at someone (or something) there is only one thing that can really stop it—an understanding of emptiness.

There is a famous story in the Tibetan scriptures of a great saint who demonstrated this high art. He was named Supar Mawa—the Poet of Peace, and he lived long, long ago in ancient India.

Supar Mawa was one of the Realized Ones, and he lived his life wandering from place to place, teaching any who were interested the path to enlightenment. One day he wandered into the forest of a certain king, in the land of Kaling.

He was sitting in the forest meditating when he heard footsteps. It was the beautiful young queen of the land. She came and humbly begged him for teachings, and he agreed and began to teach her.

But soon they were interrupted by the hunting party of the king. This king was no great spiritual person, so he did not understand seeing his new young wife alone with a male in the forest.

In fact, even in present-day India, this would normally be unheard of. The king's blood was already hot from the hunt, and he immediately became furious. He ordered the man taken and staked down to the ground. And then he ordered each of his limbs cut off, one by one, starting with the very tips of his fingers and toes and working inward, so that he would die slowly.

And what was this great saint, this Realized One, thinking as he went through hour upon hour of excruciating pain? Not a single thought of anger or resentment towards the King ever crossed his mind. Not one negative thought about how he was unfairly accused. For he knew for certain where this terrible injustice and pain was coming from—it was of course caused by he himself making a similar rash judgment and causing similar pain to someone else in the past.

Can anyone ever do anything at all to harm us? When you start to understand how absolutely everything you ever experience is from a seed that you yourself planted in the past, you realize that the answer is no. The only harm that ever comes to us is harm that we have inflicted upon ourselves. That certainly changes things. So then the mere idea of blaming someone else becomes silly. As the famous Indian master Shantideva says: "It's like blaming the stick for hitting you."

If someone came up and hit you with a stick, would you ever blame the stick? Of course not, because it's not the stick's fault—the stick is being impelled by another force. But the person wielding the stick is the same—he or she is also being impelled by another force, the force of your own past violence. This is the view we must hold in our mind if we want to get rid of anger.

The trick is that wisdom and ignorance can't exist simultaneously in the same mind. To be angry is necessarily to be in ignorance. So all we have to do is to fill our minds with wisdom—understanding how things are really coming to us—and we won't ever have to get angry again.

Imagine what life would be like, living in a mind that had no anger. There would be a peace inside your heart, a tranquility that no one could ever take from you. Once you start learning how to control your mind, and that includes controlling your emotions, you realize that this ability is really a kind of power. It is something the king could never take away from Master Supar Mawa, no matter what he did to him.

Our minds are so out of control right now—we waste so much energy and time letting ourselves be swayed this way and that by outer forces. Learn to master the inside, and then all the outside stuff will be automatically taken care of.

There is another, very serious reason for needing to control our anger, and that has to do with the results that ripple out into our world. Stop and think for a minute: where does all the violence we ever see or hear about come from? All the wars? They too are a projection, coming from our own minds; and every single act of violence you ever see or hear about comes from the small angers and violence that we do to others each day.

For you see, it all adds up, and small seeds planted grow into a great forest of trees. We must learn to control ourselves. We must stop all the pain of violence—both to still our minds, and to bring peace to the world. Here's how we do it.

MEDITATION

Killing Our Anger

◇ Get into a comfortable position, then relax your body into stillness.

◇ Let your eyes fall closed, and then focus on your breath for a few moments, to get the mind settled.

◇ Now call to mind the last time you got upset, or angry. Replay the event in your mind, so that it is as if you were right there again.

◇ Watch yourself from a distance then, and check into your mind. Find the wrong view you were holding onto that allowed the anger to arise—watch yourself blaming *someone else* for something unpleasant that is happening to you.

◇ Here is the crucial moment: now, call to mind a pure view, and remember how everything you are experiencing comes from seeds you planted in the past.

◇ Let yourself think back in time to a specific negative action you did to someone else in the past that could have been responsible for this present situation. Allow yourself a moment of regret, knowing the pain it's causing in the present.

◇ Now put yourself back in the scenario, but with these pure thoughts in mind, and then let the scenario unfold differently—watch yourself *not getting angry* this time.

◇ Feel a sense of true power, that you know what caused this, and in the future you know how to change it. You are no longer swayed by outside events—you are their master.

◇ This meditation is especially helpful with "problem" individuals in our life—people who always seem to make us angry. You can practice on your cushion, and then watch to see what effects it has in your outside life.

◇ This view takes practice—it is difficult to remember it in the heat of the moment. When you first start out, you are likely to remember it about 30 minutes *after* you have already gotten angry. But then the time gap starts to shorten, until one day you are about to open your mouth to yell back, but you remember the view and calmly close it, and smile.

19
Archetypes

There is another way to do this meditation, in a more visual form. The Tibetans are masters of the visual image, for they understand how the mind thinks. Our minds start out by picturing things, and only after do they formulate the words. Images are at the bottom of every thought, like an icon, or metaphor. It is similar in nature to what happens when we dream—we don't dream in words, we dream in pictures, and the pictures are codes that represent the things we are thinking about.

We could in fact equate this to our entire "outer world" experience—it is all just a bunch of different pictures our mind is creating, images of the thoughts inside our mind. If we looked deeply enough into any of them, we could see right through to the mind itself.

The great meditation masters of the past have "cracked the code," so to speak—they have figured out the meaning of all the different images, and how to use each of them in meditation.

I'll give you an example. In a dream, if you saw a woman in a red dress, it would signify something quite different than if you saw a woman wearing white. The very basic colors that appear all around us, that we think nothing of, are laden with meaning.

I think the great western psychologist Carl Jung was headed in this same direction with his exploration of the archetype. My Lama and I always joke about how in every country we travel to, we run into the same person in a different disguise. And it's true—if you look back on your life, you may start to see a pattern—certain roles that were always there, played by slightly different faces. And within this pattern lies all the different aspects of your own mind.

The next meditation utilizes this pattern, evoking a certain particular archetype lying hidden within us all. It is a visualization of a particular Angel, one specialized in helping us get rid of the demon of our anger. The Angel is a metaphor, yes, but She is also real—as real as you yourself sitting here now. Call on Her, and She will come and help you.

MEDITATION

The Lady Who Stops War

◇   Get into a comfortable seated position. Let your
    eyes fall closed, and your body fall still.

◇   Watch your breath for a few moments, as it exits and
    then enters your nostrils.

◇   In the space in front of you, picture a glorious wrathful
    Angel. She is ten feet tall, body the color of a midnight
    sky, with blazing red eyes and fangs that drip blood.
    She is glaring down at you fiercely, playing with the
    different weapons she holds in her hands.

◇   She is the Lady Who Stops War, and She is here
    because you called Her to help you get rid of your
    anger.

◇   She feeds on violence, death, destruction, taking it
    into Herself and destroying it forever. To Her, it is
    pure nectar.

◇ Look now into your heart, and find any anger that remains there. Look back into your recent past and recall any incidents of anger or upsetness.

◇ See them all as a charred black pile of soot in your heart.

◇ Take the whole evil black pile, and offer it now to the Angel. You have no more need of this, be rid of it— ask the Angel to destroy it for you.

◇ She takes it all, and in one swoop swallows the entire thing, reveling in it, destroying it.

◇ Your heart is now light, free of all violence or anger.

◇ Send out this Angel now, into the world, wherever there is anger, war or violence. Watch Her as She goes to each place, and swallows the anger in each person's heart, leaving only peace.

◇ Continue this until you can picture a world without any violence at all, a world in total harmony.

◇ Then thank the Angel as She flies back to Her heaven.

IV.

Shi-Ne:
Stillness

20
A Single Point

Now is what we've been doing so far really meditation? Depends on how you define it. In India, they don't call it meditation until you reach a level of deep meditative absorption. A level where you are immersed in your object so deeply that the whole world disappears.

Once I was in India, meditating in a temple with my Lama. There were some Indian holy men in the temple doing some prayers, and they started gossiping about us in Hindi (a common thing to do in temples): "No I don't think they are in meditation. I don't think they've gone beyond basic contemplation." I started to get defensive, but then I realized that if I was hearing this whole conversation and trying to focus on my object, then they were probably right!

What we've been doing up to now they'd simply call contemplation. But the Tibetans, they are so kind. They had this thought: why don't we call them meditators right from the very beginning? That way we'll plant imprints in their mind to see themselves that way, and they will reach this deep meditative absorption much faster. And it's true. It is similar to the idea of divine pride that we talked about earlier. So from now on, you are a meditator—don't ever forget! But what's it like to reach that level where we are really meditating?

Let's do an experiment: close your eyes, and place all your focus on a single point—that spot at the tip of your nose. Just stay there unmoving, and watch as the breath flows out of your body and then back in. Try to stay focused there without a single other thought, for the length of ten breaths. (Go ahead—stop reading for a second and try it.)

Could you do it? Ten breaths is about a minute, depending on how fast you breathe. If we are really honest with ourselves, if we are really watching our mind as it tries to stay on the object, we will realize that we can't stay on a single point for more that a couple of seconds—maybe three breaths. No matter how hard we try, no matter how much we want to, we simply cannot make our mind do what we want it to do.

The object of meditation is the breath. There should be no other object besides the breath coming into your mind. No thoughts like: "It's hot in here," or "I need to finish that thing," or "I wonder what's for dinner?" Because what we are striving for is a *single-pointed focus*—a totally still mind, fixed on one single object for a designated period of time.

You see, the mind can't focus on two things at the same time. You may think you are watching the breath and simultaneously wondering about dinner, but what is actually happening is a very quick toggle of the mind, from one object to another. And this micro-toggling that we do all day, it doesn't promote a still, calm mind; quite the opposite in fact—it tires our minds out.

Tibetans say there are four kinds of sustenance that a person requires in order to live: food, sleep, hope, and concentration. Concentration is like a food for the mind—it rejuvenates the mind the way a good night's sleep does for the body. I am afraid that in this society of ours we may be concentration-deprived. All that web surfing, all that constant toggle toggle toggle, is making it impossible for us to have the vibrant, alert, creative minds that we want to have. No matter how much sleep we get.

We want the waters of our mind to be as smooth as glass, so we can see right down to the bottom to the truth beneath.

We want to be so single-pointedly focused on our breath that we are no longer aware of the room we're sitting in. If someone was sitting next to us and made a noise, we'd be so focused on our object that we wouldn't even hear it.

We would be so focused that we wouldn't be aware of any other parts of our body—it would be as if everything else except the tip of your nose completely disappeared.

We wouldn't even be aware of ourselves watching the breath, because that would still be two points of focus. No, it would simply be breath. We would simply be the breath.

And time may pass, and you wouldn't notice, and yet it would be the clearest, sharpest, most aware state of mind you've ever experienced. That crystal clear state of mind is what they call stillness.

Imagine spending all your life in a dark closet, and then one day opening the door and bathing in the light of the sun for the first time. This is how it feels to reach a state of stillness. Take any physical or mental pleasure you've ever experienced up to now—this is a hundred times better. After you reach stillness, all other experiences will seem like restless agitation in comparison.

I'm sure there are moments in your life where you've come close to this depth of concentration. Great musicians, for instance, will often get so caught up in the music they are playing that they forget the entire world.

Most often it coincides with having a passion for something. If you have that passion, you can throw your mind completely into what you are doing. We need to find that passion for meditation.

21

A Single Purpose

Why is it so important to learn how to really meditate? It's not because it feels so great—that is merely a by-product. Rather, it is because every great step in our spiritual progress happens in a deep state of meditation. And there is one step in particular that we all must strive to reach.

We've talked a little about the true nature of our reality—how everything around us is a projection, how it is empty of having any nature of its own. And intellectually you grasped the concept, at least a little bit—you understood the words I wrote on the page. You formed a picture in your mind of what I was talking about.

And then, when you start to meditate on emptiness, you will start to have a deeper and deeper understanding of it. The mental image that comes to mind when someone says "emptiness" will become more and more elaborate. But it is still only a conceptual understanding—it is still only a mental picture which represents the thing, and not the thing itself.

I'll give you an example. It is as if someone were explaining to you what an atom was. First they told you: "It is the building block of all material things," and you got a vague picture of the chair you were sitting on made up of lots of tiny round things too small to see. Then they explained about protons and neutrons and electrons, and your mental picture of it got more elaborate.

But then one day, you looked into a microscope and saw one for yourself, and something changed. What you had been taking pretty much on faith up to this point was now there before your very eyes. That was the day atoms became real for you.

We need to make emptiness real for us. We need to see it directly. That is the only way to our goal—the only way to evolve from this impure body and mind that has pain and gets old and dies, to a Being of total purity, with a bliss-filled body of light and mind filled with nothing but love. A Being who is no longer fettered to one single time or place, but who can be in all places and at all times simultaneously.

You see, we need to understand that this body and mind of ours, they too are empty—really both of them are simply concepts, images. Just another projection. What that means is that this body and this mind are infinitely changeable. We are not stuck within the limitations that life has doled out to us. We can create a different projection. Stop and let yourself dream for a minute what it would be like, to see yourself not as you are now, but as One who has reached the ultimate goal. Making it happen is as simple as a shift in our perception.

But right now it is hard to imagine. Our belief in our current body and mind is so strong—we are so attached to these impure ideas of our "self"—that we cannot break free, we cannot change, until we see firsthand for ourselves just what they really are, and what they are not, and what they could be.

So we must get to a level of deep meditative stillness, because that is the platform on which we can see emptiness directly. And seeing emptiness directly will rock your entire world.

22

Seeing Emptiness Directly

Until you see emptiness directly, you have never had a correct perception. Everything you have ever experienced is in some way a lie. Because it all seems to be really out there. We talked a little about the difference between concepts and a direct experience. Well, what if I were to tell you you've never had a direct experience—that it is all a bunch of concepts—a series of pictures in your mind.

There are two realities. There is the one we are living in now, experienced through the world of our sense powers, and that is called "deceptive" reality, because it is constantly fooling us. Then underneath all that illusion is what they call "ultimate" reality—the true nature of all existing things.

When you go into the direct perception of emptiness, you are in direct communion with ultimate reality for the first time. It is a state completely beyond this world, it is what the Tibetans call judu mepa—

impossible to describe in words. But we can say it's like being in the presence of the true face of God. Pure, unadulterated truth. You have left the senses long behind— there is no more seeing, hearing, and the rest. You have also left yourself behind—there is no more perception of a body or mind. No perception of time or space. Because all those things are objects of deceptive reality. So what's left to see?

Imagine someone who was blind from birth. Could you describe to them what the color red is like? Now imagine what it would feel like if this person were suddenly cured and could see. It is as if a whole new realm is revealed.

Once you come out of seeing emptiness directly, you are thrown into a subsequent series of realizations. You realize what you saw, and that it was the ultimate truth. So there's no way someone could see emptiness directly and not be sure. If you see it, you know. You understand truly for the first time that you are going to die, and that this life is pain, because you actually see your death. But you also realize who you will soon become—this great evolution into a Being of light, all because of what you saw. And you realize what steps you have to take to get there as quickly as possible. So what you are going to do with the rest of your life is now crystal clear—you know what you have to do.

When you come out of seeing emptiness, you are once again forced to see things wrongly—things once again appear to be "out there," coming from their own side. But the difference is that now you know, now you can no longer be fooled. And because of that you are free.

You are now a different kind of person. You are what they call a Realized One—someone who has no more fear.

23
Getting to Stillness

Now that we've got the goal clearly in mind, we can get to work on the method: meditation. Meditation is hard for us westerners, because we haven't ever trained our minds, and so they are like jello—weak and flabby. Forget minutes. We are not even on the object for more than a few seconds before the mind starts jumping off to something else. We have no mental muscles built up to hold our mind in place. It's like someone who has spent their whole life as a couch potato, and then tries to take a jog around the block—very difficult! But if that same person does that same jog every day, it becomes easier and easier. You get the point.

After I met the young monks in the monastery, I was so embarrassed at the undisciplined state of my mind. Twelve years old, and they could run mental circles around me! But besides humility, I learned something else very important. We are living way below our potential. We have grown up without having ever really been challenged, and we have no idea of our capacity. Not only is this a huge disservice to humanity, it is just plain boring if we don't continue to push ourselves to learn and grow. It is never too late to start. I started my training eighteen years later than these little monks normally do.

Just make the commitment. Resolve to yourself that you will do it—you will push yourself and reach this place of stillness.

24
Not Doing It

So how do we get to that beautiful state—how do we make our mind still?

Tibetans say there are six things you must overcome in order to get to that really deep state of single-pointed focus on our object. They call them the six obstacles to meditation. The first one is so obvious that it would be funny, if it weren't so insidious. For this first obstacle is the toughest one—it can get in your way even after you have become pretty good at meditation. (Sometimes even after 20 years!)

So what is the biggest of meditation demons? Not doing it! Everyone will agree that if don't actually sit down on your cushion, you are definitely not going to make any progress. But we are all so busy, and there are so many things out there to distract us from just sitting down and meditating.

We must make the idea of sitting on that cushion the most alluring, attractive thing we can imagine. We must convince ourselves how much we truly want to meditate today. And the next, and the next. Then finding the time will be easy. We can always find the time to do the things we really want to do.

So how do we convince ourselves? Just keep imagining what it will be like when you yourself reach those deep states of concentration we talked about earlier.

Let yourself dream about who you want to become and how just a few minutes on the cushion each day is going to get you there. Then sit down, and watch; it's already starting to happen.

25
Losing the Object

When most of us first sit down to meditate, we have this very shocking realization—the mind doesn't do what I want it to! We experience for the first time what the Tibetans jokingly call the "monkey mind"—a mind totally out of control, jumping from here to there without a moment's rest. We plan to meditate on a certain topic, but instead most of the time is spent thinking of something completely different.

Or, even when our minds are not totally flying off, still we can't get the object straight—you might start to meditate on a figure in red, but yellow pops up instead! It can be a little discouraging, until you realize that everyone goes through this at the beginning. For this is the second big obstacle to meditation: losing the object.

What it means is that we've gone through our whole lives without ever really trying to control our mind, just letting our thoughts come and go at will. There's no magic formula for fixing this particular problem. The solution is plain, day-to-day effort: a two-step process of slowly training the mind to do what you want it to do.

Step #1: Whenever your mind flies off, the first important step is to catch it in the act, to notice that it has happened. To think: "Oh, I am no longer on the object." This itself is a skill you will get better and better at as the days and weeks go by—there will be a shorter and shorter lag time between the point where the mind has flown off and the point where you notice that it has.

Step #2: Pull the mind back to the original object. This is often difficult to do, since our mind will naturally wander off to objects we find attractive in some way. Be strict! Don't let that monkey get the better of you: rein him in, and train him that you're not going to let him get away with this wild behavior anymore. "Sit! Stay." Be the boss of your own mind, for at least a few minutes a day.

Now you start to get the feeling of being a little schizophrenic. Who am I anyway—the mind, or the one who is pulling the mind back? If you want to meditate well, you will have to develop this new alter ego. I like to call him the Watcher—this little policeman inside that is watching the mind, and then pulling it out of trouble. We will need the services of this Watcher all the way up to the level of perfect meditative stillness.

One interesting question: can you watch the Watcher? Try it and see for yourself. If you come to the conclusion that you can, then there has to be another Watcher watching the first. And if that is true, then depending on your state of concentration there could be infinite Watchers—just like the infinite drops in infinite hearts that we talked about before.

The mind is truly a wondrous place.

MEDITATION

Breath Meditation

Here is a meditation that every Tibetan does for a few minutes before going into their main meditation. It is the very simple exercise of watching the breath. Now just sitting down and watching our breath for hours on end is not going to lead us to see emptiness directly—there is not much to be gained by doing that. We use it mainly to put the mind in a neutral space—an intermediate state between our outer life and our inner one—an exercise that prepares the mind for going into a deeper state.

Breath meditation is also a good barometer for us. We can use it to check each day where our mind is. It is interesting to note a correlation between how well you watch your breath in the morning and how well the rest of your day goes. Even more interesting is the correlation between how well you watch your breath and how you behaved towards others the day before.

If you pay close enough attention, you can figure out exactly what agitates the mind, and what makes it still. Then getting to single-pointed concentration will be easy.

Part 1

◇ Get into a comfortable position, close your eyes, and then let your body fall still and silent.

◇ Focus now at the tip of your nose, watching the air as it first flows out, and then back into the body.

◇ Begin to count the breaths as you watch: the exhale is the first half of the breath, and then the inhale is the second half, making one whole breath.

◇ Try to keep your mind fixed on that single object of watching your breath at the tip of your nose, for a total of ten breaths.

◇ If you lose your focus or your mind jumps to something else for a minute, start the count over at one.

◇ As you practice this day by day, see if you can steadily increase your focus until you really can get up to the ten breaths without a single other thought interrupting.

Part 2

◇ Place all your focus on hearing the sound of the breath as it exits and then enters the body. Listen for ten breaths. Don't try to make the breath any louder; instead make your focus sharper.

◇ Now switch your focus a little bit: instead of hearing the breath, just try to feel it. Focus on the feeling at that same point at the tip of the nose as it exits and enters the body. Feel how it is warm going out and cool coming in. See if you can just feel the breath without visualizing anything, as you feel another ten breaths.

◇ Return to visualizing the breath, but this time incorporate hearing it and feeling it as well. Focus on all three together for ten more breaths.

Which one was easiest for you to focus on? It is different for everyone. But one thing to remember: when someone tells you to focus on an object, it doesn't just mean a visual image. Try to incorporate as many senses into the meditation as you can—bring it to life.

One thing you will notice as you do the meditation—when the Tibetans count their breaths, they do it backwards. What I mean is, they start with the exhale first, and then end with the inhale to make one full breath. There are very profound reasons for doing it this way, which we can discuss later, but all you need to know for now is that it serves to calm the mind.

MEDITATION TIP

STILL AS STONE

We talked about the seat you should take, and how to position your body for meditation, but we haven't yet talked about the most important aspect—how to sit and be still.

The body is simply another layer of mind—a grosser, outer layer. So we can look to our body to see what state our mind is in. Is the mind slouching? Is the mind too rigid and tense? We use the body as an outer reflection of the mind, to check on its condition.

But we can also work backwards— we can use the grosser layer to affect the more subtle one. For instance, if we hold our body perfectly still, the mind becomes still as well.

It's quite simple. Since we cannot hope to reach a state of mental stillness while our body is squirming about, we need to perfect the *art of sitting still.*

There is a deep stillness that settles into the body during any good meditation. It is rather like the state your body falls into when you dream. During the dream state, your glands send a chemical throughout the body that freezes it to stone, so that you don't start walking around acting out your dreams while you sleep. During meditation you have to send this message—you have to train the body to freeze itself into stone.

Here now is a meditative practice for learning how to reach this stillness of body.

◇ Settle into your favorite most comfortable meditation posture.

◇ Let your eyes fall closed, and watch your breath for a few moments.

◇ Focus first now on feeling your body as a whole, as it sits there in meditation. Feel that it has been frozen in space, just like a statue—without any movement whatsoever.

◇ Send a message to your body—let the idea of stillness wash over your entire form. Then throughout the practice, no matter what happens, don't allow yourself to move even the slightest bit. Let your body relax into the posture, and feel the weight of your body as it sinks down into the floor.

◇ Now go step-by-step through each and every part of your outer form from the tip of the head down to your toes, letting it fall deeper into body stillness.

◇ Turn your gaze to the inside of the body, and see it as completely empty inside, just a hollow shell, the color of the clear blue sky.

◇ Then go step-by-step through every inch of this hollow space inside your inner form, from the toes up to the tip of the head, making sure you see nothing but empty sky.

This is a great exercise to do just before you begin your main meditation. One word of advice—make sure you don't spend too long on it, or you'll tire yourself out before the main event!

26

Dullness

Are you getting sleepy? Or perhaps just a little bored? The Tibetans call this problem dullness, and it can range from the inability to keep yourself from snoring, on up to a very subtle lack of intensity in your focus.

Really extreme cases are easy to deal with. If you are falling asleep during your meditation, it most likely means that you simply haven't slept enough the night before. You must get as much sleep as your own body needs, in order to have any kind of quality meditation. And this will vary from person to person, so you have to listen to your own body and be the judge.

Another sure way to get really dull-minded and sleepy is to eat too much, or to eat right before meditating. You don't want to meditate just after you've eaten, because all the body's energy goes to your stomach to digest the food, so you literally can't think so well. Leave at least an hour between eating and meditation, and if it was a big meal, perhaps a little longer. What kinds of foods you eat will also affect your meditation.

Once you become a meditator, you are no longer eating just because it tastes good, you are eating to provide the necessary energy—fuel for your body and mind. So you must pay attention. If you wake up and have a really groggy meditation, think: what did I eat last night for dinner? Keep track of all the foods that work for you and those that don't. Every body is different, in the end it is up to you to listen to your body and figure out what is right for you.

Also there's nothing worse for your meditation than getting upset the day before. It is just plain exhausting whenever some negative thought or emotion attacks you and temporarily takes over your mind. So now you as a meditator must do everything you possibly can to avoid getting upset.

The best way to combat a state of extreme dullness is to simply avoid ever getting into that state of mind in the first place, by avoiding all the pitfalls I've listed above. But if you do happen to find yourself there, here are a couple of desperation fixes to try to use in the moment.

The mind at this point is dark, you can even say a little depressed. A good solution is simply to picture something physically bright, like the bright light of the sun in the sky. Or you can uplift the mind by thinking of something mentally bright, something happy, like the face of someone you love, or how beautiful you are going to look when you evolve into an angel Being of Light.

You need to know yourself well enough to choose something that you are sure will bring your mind out of those murky depths. One tip: at the moment when you are feeling this dull-minded, it will be difficult to think of anything at all, so prepare your happy antidote thought ahead of time—decide now what it is going to be.

That was the overt form of dullness. They sometimes call it lethargy. It is very clear when you have it, and there are fairly obvious remedies for it. The really insidious problem is subtle dullness.

The terrible thing about subtle dullness is that you might not know you have it. You are sitting perfectly still, and your mind is fixed on the object for an extended period of time. Moreover, the object is very clear. But there is an energy behind it which is missing. People may go on meditating like this for years, never reaching the bliss of true meditative absorption, because they fail to detect this one nasty little problem.

When you are really immersed in your object, there is an excitement about it, a passion for it. It is the same feeling you get when you are watching a really amazing movie—you are totally immersed in the story, totally swept away. You need to develop this same feeling about your meditation object: on the edge of your seat, engaged.

Tibetans use the word ngar, which translates as intensity, but can also mean the razor-sharp edge of a knife. Your mind needs to be razor sharp. You need to push your concentration up a notch, and then another, and then another—until your mind is gripping the object as firmly as it can without bouncing off the object altogether. But we'll talk about that later.

The very best way to reach that passion, that intensity of focus on your meditation object, is to pick an object that truly interests you, one that is a joy to be with every day. Something that makes you look forward to being on your cushion. That requires a bit of imaginative work on your part. I am providing the basic structure of the meditations; now it's your job to make them really interesting.

27

Agitation

Agitation is the other extreme.

Just as with dullness, there is an overt form of agitation, and then there is a more subtle form.

Overt agitation I like to call restlessness. It is that uncomfortable state where you are squirming around here and there, opening your eyes to peek at the clock, to see just how long you have to go before you can get up off the cushion. Or even if you do manage to keep your body still and not look at the clock, you're still thinking about it. Your mind is darting here and there, even as you watch your object, in an incessant micro-toggle.

You're thinking about all the things you have to do today. You're thinking about what that person said yesterday. You're planning how to bump into that cute boy or girl again. Your mind is interested in anything except your meditation object. It's a constant stream of useless dialogue.

Why can't you focus? Because you've forgotten why you are sitting there in the first place. The mind is too busy, too hyper—you need to bring it down, like reeling in a kite that's too far up in the clouds and is getting out of control.

The antidote? Think about someone you know who is in pain, and how you need to do this for them. Think about your own coming death, and how it could happen at any moment. Remind yourself why you started meditating in the first place. You need to come up with a very personal solution—something you know will ground you, take your mind out of the clouds and bring you back to earth.

Then when you feel your mind is sufficiently grounded, you can try going back to your original object of meditation and see if your focus is better.

That is the solution for a restless mind.

The subtle form of agitation is where your mind is steadily on the object, but underneath that there are some other thoughts running in the background. It is like when the surface of a river has frozen, but there is still moving water running underneath the ice.

The solution for this problem is interesting. What's happening is that your mind is locked a bit too tightly on the object, and so actually you need to loosen up a bit. Relax the mind, just a bit. Too much, and you'll be headed off into subtle dullness.

We want our minds to be exactly in the middle, right between dullness and agitation. When we are just beginners, we try to apply the antidote for dullness, and we push too far, so that we end up with agitation, or vice versa. We need to learn to measure exactly just how far to push our minds in either direction, in order to reach that perfect state of balance between the two. And that simply takes a bit of practice. It is all a beautiful process of watching and learning your own mind.

Some people possess a personality type which is naturally prone to dullness, and so they will have to learn to push harder to reach that point of intensity in their meditation. Other people are more prone to agitation, and the hardest thing for them will be to learn how to relax. But once you get there, you'll realize that this middle-way state of mind is much more pleasant, and you can learn to apply it outside of meditation as well.

Another tip: since the body and mind are so integrally connected, if you are feeling habitually dull you may want to try lifting your chin up just a bit; or if your main problem is agitation you may try bringing your chin a touch toward your chest. You may even find that when you are having agitation the chin has raised itself up from where you put it at the beginning, or vice versa—another thing to watch out for as you watch your mind.

28

Stillness on the Lama

Tibetans always insist that one of the best ways to reach a state of stillness is to meditate on your holy spiritual teacher.

When I first traveled to India, and when I was staying at the monastery in Nepal, everyone I met kept telling me I needed to find a spiritual teacher. I kept putting this advice aside, thinking: "I'll just do it myself." But after I came home and lost so much of what I thought I had learned, I realized that I couldn't actually do it by myself—that I needed help. Thus I began in my heart to search for a qualified spiritual guide: what they call a "Lama" in Tibet, or a "Guru" in India.

In the West we are very skeptical of such things, for we have not been raised in a culture which values humility and service. We are afraid of being "taken advantage of"—afraid of losing our independence, our identity. But there are certain things that simply can't be learned without a little surrender.

Let me try to explain to you a little about the relationship of spiritual teacher to student. It is like an apprenticeship: in the old days, when you wished to be a blacksmith, you found a master blacksmith. You went to him and said: "Let me work for you for free for 6 to 12 years. I'll do all the dirty work: I'll fetch the water, I'll clean up—just teach me what you know. All you have to give me is a few meals a day and a place to sleep."

And so the master says okay and trains you, and you watch and learn until you become as good as the master himself. Then one day he kicks you out of the nest and tells you to go start your own blacksmith shop. And you do. Now you are the master blacksmith. Then inevitably sooner or later a young boy or girl comes to you to be trained. And by then you realize that having an apprentice is more trouble for you than help, but because someone in the past has shown you kindness and trained you, you feel you must repay it by passing on the knowledge to someone else. So you agree, and the lineage continues on.

This is the system of passing on knowledge from teacher to student that has gone on in Tibet for centuries—one that has worked to preserve not only the book knowledge, but actual realizations in the hearts and minds of those who choose to enter this relationship. It is a beautiful process of truly learning something deeply, a tradition that I feel may be getting lost in the world.

Who is a Lama? What do they look like? How do I find one? A Lama can be anyone—man, woman, or child—of any race or creed. You might find that you mom is your Lama, or your high school boyfriend. The only qualification is that it must be someone whom you admire, someone you learn from, someone you wish to become. It can be someone far away or very close to you. It can even be someone who has already passed from this world, like Mother Theresa or Mahatma Gandhi. But one thing to remember: the closer they are to you, the faster you progress. So picking your spouse or child or parent as a Lama can be a very wise choice.

Why is it faster? Because it makes you work harder. Once you take someone as a Lama, it is then your job to try and see everything they do as a special teaching just for you. That's pretty easy if they are so far away you never see them. But if they live with you, well, that's a different matter entirely.

People always ask if they can have more than one Lama. Of course! The more people you see that way, the better. I'll even tell you a secret: after a while your mind gets so pure that everyone starts to appear to be a Lama, moving through the world just to teach you. And who's to say they are not?

MEDITATION

Lama Meditation

◇ Take a comfortable position, close your eyes, and focus on your breath for a minute to get the mind settled.

◇ Now picture just in front of you the most beautiful Holy Being you can imagine. This is your spiritual guide, your Lama, in their most divine form.

◇ Their body is made of light, softly glowing. Fill in every detail about their face, their posture, their dress. Try to feel the warmth from their body, and the pure sweet smell that radiates from them.

◇ They are gazing down at you with the deepest love for you; they are so happy to be with you.

◇ See that this light pouring from their holy body is simply a manifestation of their incredible love for all creatures.

◇ Believe that this angel is really sitting in front of you. Look into their eyes and be with them for a while, in stillness.

◇ Try to hold your mind fixed on this Being in front of you—don't let it wander anywhere else. Use your heart and all of your senses. The more real they are for you, the easier it will be.

◇ To close the meditation, first make them an offering to thank them for coming. Offer them the wish to have that same kind of love in your heart; offer them the wish to become an angel like them.

◇ The angel hears your request, and slowly rises up in the air before you. They turn to face the same direction that you are facing, and then start to shrink down smaller and smaller, until they are just a tiny ball of light.

◇ The ball of angel light comes to rest at the top of your head, then slowly dissolves down into your body, coming to rest inside your heart.

29

When to Take Action

One problem that arises after we've been meditating for a good period of time is a different kind of laziness. It's not that you don't want to do your meditation—you are there, on your cushion, focused on your object. You have gotten to the point where you are no longer losing the object. And you are comfortable where you are mentally, so comfortable in fact that you don't want to push yourself to work harder—to actually reach a state of complete stillness.

So maybe some subtle agitation is there in the background, or maybe some subtle dullness has crept in, but you don't do anything about it. This is the meditation obstacle that the ancient texts call "not taking the necessary action."

Of course you know the solution: don't just sit there, do something about it!

It is often simply a case of letting the Watcher mind slide: of thinking that you don't need him anymore. Trust me, we need him, all the way to stillness. It's usually not a conscious decision; our diligence just naturally tends to loosen up after time.

There is a great technique that helps us avoid this problem altogether. It is called "tracking our meditation."

Invest in a small journal, and keep it beside your meditation cushion (tucked out of sight during meditation, of course). Every time you end a meditation, take out the journal and write just a few sentences about how the meditation went.

First jot down the date, time and length of the meditation. Then write a one-line description of the general subject of the meditation. Next, write down the amount of time you were on the object. Example: "I meditated for 30 minutes, and was on the object for about 20 minutes."

After that, write down the quality of the meditation. Example: "I was slightly sleepy in the beginning, then my mind sharpened up. Focus was generally clear."

Lastly, make a note of something that you learned from the meditation. It can be anything from a profound realization to a helpful meditation tip for yourself. Example: "Used an extra cushion, which helped my knees. Tried to meditate after lunch, which caused some sleepiness in the beginning."

That's it. Keep it short and simple—that way it will be easy to do, just one extra minute after the meditation ends. Simply writing these things down will encourage you to keep watch of your mind during your meditations.

Your meditation journal serves another purpose as well—as a way to chart how your meditation has progressed over time. Every once

JAN 22 2010 6 AM - 6:30 AM
SUBJECT: LAMA MEDITATION
TIME: I MEDITATED 30 MINUTES
& WAS ON OBJECT 15 . . MTRS
QUALITY: In the beginning I
kept thinking of a project
I was working on, but
eventually my mind
became focused and
I felt a sweet sense
of peace.
LEARNED: I became more
focused when I just
concentrated on my
Lama eyes and
nothing else.

in a while, take out one of your old meditation journals and browse through it. You may be surprised how far you've come.

Here's a chart describing what the Tibetans call the "Nine Stages of Meditation." It is always nice to be able to pinpoint what level you've reached in your meditation. You can tell all your friends: "I've reached meditation stage number four!"

The 9 Stages of Meditation

Stage #1: Placing an object in your mind

You have learned the instructions, and are on the road at last.

Stage #2: Bringing the mind back

Your monkey mind at this point keeps forgetting what it is doing, and you spend more time off the object than on it.

Stage #3: Bridging the gaps

Your mind now stays mostly on its object, with only brief patches where it wanders.

Stage #4: Holding tight

Here your mind stays on the object without wandering at all.

Stage #5: Discipline

You win the battle against agitation!

Stage #6: Getting Quiet\Quieting Down

You conquer mental dullness!

Stage #7: Completely Calm

Now you have control over the subtlest forms of dullness or agitation!

Stage #8: Single-Pointed

Just a tiny bit of effort, and you're there.

Stage #9: Perfect Balance

Effortless, like breathing.

30
Letting Go

The last meditation problem is actually sort of sweet—you have become so good at trying to watch your mind, and trying to balance it between dullness and agitation, that you continue to do so even after there is no longer any need for it.

You have reached a state where your mind has found a perfect balance. Now all you have to do is leave things alone. Just let go—put the Watcher to rest and let yourself become totally immersed in the grace of your perfect meditation. You'll know when you are there.

31
Reaching Stillness

After you have mastered the high art of letting go, and you reach
that stage where deep, balanced meditation comes as easily as breath
itself, something happens within you. All the inner flows of your body
fall into perfect alignment. And when this happens, it sends you into
a state of physical and mental bliss. A quiet kind of bliss – something
akin to total peace. When you feel this, you'll know you've reached
stillness.

V.

Tong~Nyi:
Emptiness

32

A Word About Emptiness

Tibetans say that misperceiving our world is the cause of all our pain. Behind every moment of sadness or frustration, anger or disappointment, there lies a kind of ignorance at its root. So if we could attack our problems at the very source; if we could rip out the very root of all our ignorance, we could be free of all pain forever.

You know the ignorance I am talking about. It is thinking that things really exist out there, from their own side—that things are coming towards you from some source other than ourselves.

And you know the solution: to attack this ignorance, we must meditate on emptiness.

The more we understand emptiness, the less upset we will get when something unexpected or unpleasant happens to us. This is because, as the ancient texts say, every kind of unhappiness of the mind (aside from healthy regret) is necessarily an ignorant state of mind. In fact, they say that any unhappy state of mind is a negative karma, because it hurts us—it plants seeds to see ourselves unhappy in the future.

So a good barometer for how your emptiness meditations are going is how upset you got the last time somebody yelled at you. And of course, if your emptiness meditations are really good, you'll understand how to fix it so there *are* no more people yelling at you.

Your meditations should always have that kind of positive effect on the rest of your life. If they are not, then something is wrong. And this is especially relevant with meditations on emptiness.

I have heard wild tales about what emptiness is, from numerous dubious sources. That it is some kind of light, that it is like outer space, that it means nothing matters. None of these are going to help you reach to a place beyond all pain. Keep on track—make sure your meditations on emptiness are making you a better person, and your world a better place.

33

Gakja: What Emptiness is Empty Of

These *objects*, these things that we *think* we are seeing all around us, are in actuality things which are completely impossible. Tibetans say that they are like the horns of a rabbit, or a flower blooming in mid-air: something that is simply impossible. And if we were truly objective, if we were strictly logical in our thinking about how the world works, then we would realize that what we are doing is ludicrous—it doesn't even match up to our own sensory experience. But we are so habituated to this incorrect way of thinking that we are blind to any inconsistencies.

The first step is catching ourselves in the act of seeing things incorrectly. The thing that we are saying is impossible is any thing which could exist in and of itself, which has its own nature, its own separate identity, apart from us. Now let's examine this for a minute. What exactly would a self-existent thing look like?

Well if something existed as itself by itself, then absolutely everyone who ever looked at it would see it exactly the same way. Because it would be self-sufficient—it wouldn't depend on anyone else's perspective. It would be a pen that even dogs or ants or a person from 4,000 years ago could see as a pen.

It wouldn't even matter if you put your glasses on or not, because the thing would always appear exactly the same way to you. In fact, you wouldn't even have to turn on a light to see it! Because something that is self-sufficient would not have to depend on a light to be visible.

If any object in the world actually had a nature of its own, then that nature would be fixed—it could never change. So no one could ever pick up a self-existent pen and use it to scratch their back, or mark their place in a book. Because that pen doesn't have any nature of being a backscratcher or a bookmark: its *only* nature is that of a pen. So actually, a pen would always have to be writing—because the nature of a pen is to write.

But a self-sufficient pen wouldn't have to depend on us in order to write—it could write all by itself!

So if it was already writing, how could we ever use it?

The truth is, it would be completely impossible to ever *interact* with any object that was self-existent. It would be in its own self-existent world, and you could never reach it. For one thing, if we ever used it, then it would be depending on us for its existence and therefore no longer be self-existent. For another thing, if we interacted with it, it would change, and would therefore no longer have a fixed nature.

Yet this is what we are claiming about every single object around us, despite every evidence to the contrary. We really *believe* that the walls around us function on their own, that they are fixed, solid things that hold up the roof above our heads—that it has absolutely nothing to do with us—when in fact, the only reason that roof doesn't come crashing down on us is because of some goodness we have done in the past.

What holds the wall together? The very atoms of the walls around us—they are made up of kindness. Kindness that you did to others in the past. (By the way, this is only the case if you like the walls. If the person next to you were claustrophobic, for them it would be a different story. More evidence that the walls have no nature of their own.)

So look around at the room you are in right now. Try to find something in that room—any little thing at all—that *doesn't* come from you, that doesn't come from how you have treated others in the past. Go ahead, really stop and do it.

Did you find anything? When you look for a self-existent thing and you come up empty-handed, *that* is emptiness.

We said earlier that emptiness is a negative thing, and that when you get an understanding of emptiness, it is this great realization that something you first thought was there is not. It is like reaching into your pocket for your wallet, and finding out that your pocket is empty. There is this sudden feeling of "Oh my gosh, it's not there!" That's where we want to get to in our understanding of emptiness.

There is a famous Tibetan named Kedrup Je, who lived during the 15th Century, and who devised a specific meditation just to get us to that "Oh my gosh it's not there" feeling. It is called "Kedrup Je's Four-Step Meditation on Emptiness."

These are four very simple steps for practicing looking for the thing we think is there, and then "Oh my gosh!" finding out that it's not.

MEDITATION

Kedrup Je's Four-Step Meditation on Emptiness

◊ Get into a comfortable position. Let the eyes fall closed, and the body fall still.

◊ Focus on your breath for a few moments, to calm the mind, watching the air flow out and then into the body.

◊ Step # 1: Picture the room you are sitting in. In your mind's eye, see everything in the room—what's on the walls, the tables, the shelves, and so on. Go carefully through from one corner of the room to the other, trying to call as much detail as possible up in your mind. Look at all these as you normally do.

◇ Step # 2: Then look with a mind of ignorance—as if they were out there, existing from their own side, through some nature of their own. This is the gakja — the impossible thing that could never exist. Take a few minutes here, and try to catch the wrong view you are constantly holding to, every minute of the day. What does it mean to think a thing is self-existent, and why is it impossible?

◇ Step # 3: Switch your view and see the same room with wisdom—see every single thing in it as a picture coming from your mind. Stay here for a few minutes, just watching yourself projecting these mental images.

◇ Step # 4: This is a crucial point. Now stop the projection—pull back whatever is coming from you and check to see what is left. What is *behind* what you are projecting? Is there any reality at all to these objects other than the reality you are giving them?

◇ When you reach step # 4 and you get that "Oh, my gosh it's not there!" feeling of absence, you know you're headed in the right direction.

Helpful Hints

As my Lama likes to say, emptiness is slippery – it is like trying to catch a fish with your bare hands. At the beginning, step #4 might be very elusive. You come to it in your mind, and for a split second you think you've grasped it, but then it slips away. At that point, go back through the first three steps again and try to bring yourself back to that glimpse of understanding. Work up to brighter and brighter glimpses, for longer and longer periods of time.

34

Cornering Emptiness

Emptiness is a tricky thing. It is difficult to grasp. For we are trying to reach something that cannot be described in words through words, something that cannot be conceptualized through concepts. But if we take these concepts, which are not emptiness itself and could never be, and we let our minds run with them, they will lead us to the actual experience.

That is why there are hundreds of thousands of pages written about this subject in the Tibetan texts. The more different perspectives you can get of this thing we call emptiness, the fuller your conception of it will be, and the closer you will be to the thing itself. So we will start to explore emptiness now from a number of different directions.

They say if your mind is really ripe, meaning if you are really ready to see emptiness, then each new description of it will send chills down your spine and you won't be able to stop thinking about it. If your mind is not so ripe, this section could very well give you a headache.

How to make your mind ripe? Ah, good question. That is the very reason for all the previous meditations in this book.

35

Things Change

> See anything
> Brought about by causes
> As like a star,
> A speck of dust in the eye,
> A lamp, an illusion,
> The dew, or a bubble;
> A dream, or lightning,
> Or else a cloud.
>> —The Diamond Cutter Sutra, 500 BC

We talked at the beginning of this book about how nothing ever lasts, how we cannot hold onto anything. There's always an end to things, whether big or small. Pens run out. Your life runs out. The Tibetans call this impermanence. And the more you understand that this is the way the world works right now in this broken realm we live in, the less upset you will get when something comes to an end. Someone's favorite cup falls to the ground and breaks in the monastery, and you can see him smile and say under his breath, "Ah, impermanence."

But when they say "things change" there is a deeper meaning, one that leads us to understand emptiness. As the famous Greek philosopher named Heroditus once said, "You never step into the same river twice." (And later when I traveled to India and went to the sacred river Ganges, all the local people were telling me the same thing. Everyone in India is a philosopher.)

The point is that the water you see and feel on Wednesday will not be the same water that you see and feel on Thursday, because *that* water will be far downstream by then. A simple concept, with profound implications.

Tibetans say that our whole world is like that: nothing we ever see is the same object that we saw yesterday, or even a moment ago— every single object is in a constant state of flux.

For one thing, with every moment that passes, the things around us are getting a little older—another moment closer to their death. With each new breath you take, your face gets another tiny wrinkle.

But going further, with every different moment that passes, we have a different experience of the object. We can never have exactly the same experience walking down a road as we did the day before.

That's why we can't ever hold onto things. They slip through our fingers like sand, because they are not static and fixed, as we think they are. They are constantly moving, like the river. It is like listening to a song—even as the song is being played, each note is appearing and disappearing with every passing moment; we can never capture them.

We'll do a little demonstration of Buddhist perceptual theory to prove my point. Identify what this is a drawing of:

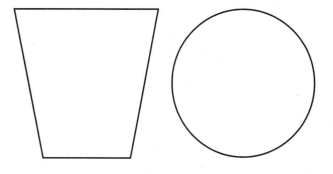

Is it a drawing of two different things? Or is it a drawing of one thing? You pretty much have to say that it's two different things. One is a circle, and the other is what they call a trapezoid (or an upside-down triangle with the bottom cut off!). Now what if you saw them sequentially: what if you saw the trapezoid in the first moment, and the circle in the second? *Then* would they be one thing or two things? How could a triangle ever turn into a circle?

Turn the page and I'll show you.

This is the first moment of the coffee cup, and this is the second moment of the cup, and so on. Images that flash by and are gone a moment later.

Stop for a moment and think about the implications of this: *what we are actually seeing does not correspond to how we view the world.* The eye sees two things, the mind sees one. But this is a problem, because the only way we ever have to confirm the existence of something outside of us is through the door of our five senses—our visual consciousness and the rest.

The mind is doing something funny to the raw data it receives from the eye.

The eye can't ever see "cup." "Cup" is a concept, an idea. It sees only colors and shapes. So our eye here picks up this trapezoid thing in the first moment, and this circle thing in the second, and it is the *mind* that comes along and superimposes the concept of "cup" onto them both. It links the two images together seamlessly to form one "object." And that's where all the cups in the world ever come from. There *are* no cups, except for the cups in your mind.

So the cup that you think you see—the one that is sitting "out there" on the kitchen table, the one that is still there when you leave the room—is a cup that doesn't even exist. It never could exist. Because if it really was out there from its own side, in the way that we've been thinking it is, then it could *never change*. You'd always see the exact same thing. And you could never drink from it!

This last point is a bit difficult; as one Tibetan Lama I knew used to tell me, "Cook it!" which always meant that I should meditate on it for a while.

So that is how we meditate on the fact that things are constantly changing, in order to bring ourselves to an understanding of the emptiness of the "things" around us.

And if we realize this—if we come to understand the constantly changing nature of our reality—then we can save ourselves a lot of pain that inevitably comes from trying to grasp onto something that is not there. Every step closer to emptiness is a step away from pain.

MEDITATION

Walking to the Door

◇ Get into a comfortable position, then relax and let the body fall still.

◇ Focus your breath for a minute or so, simply watching the air as it flows out and in.

◇ Now, we are going to attack our misconceptions about *things*—we are going to challenge our belief that the objects around us are static and unchanging.

◇ Picture in your mind the door to the room you are sitting in. Observe how you think it exists—as a solid, fixed thing out there, a certain distance away from you.

◇ Now picture yourself getting up and walking towards the door. Go all the way to the point when you open it.

◇ Play this picture back again in your mind, like a movie. What is happening to the door? It is getting bigger and bigger with every step you take.

◇ Now simplify the picture for a moment—take away some of the overlays and interpretations of the mind, and try to focus on just what the eye is seeing, moment by moment. The eye sees a small rectangle, then a slightly bigger one, then an even bigger one, and so on—flashes of still images in a rapid sequence, just like the frames of a movie.

◇ How many different doors does the eye see?

◇ Then what does the mind do with all these different images? The mind comes and glues all these separate pictures together, and calls them a "door."

◇ Picture yourself walking to the door again, only this time, shift your perception: see it as if it were passing frames of a movie—a projection of a sequence of images within your own virtual reality.

◇ You can never walk to the door, because there *is* no door as you are seeing it—no static, fixed single *thing,* because that could never change. Try to get to a feeling of absence about the door you thought was there.

◇ Now try this same meditation on any other object in the room.

◇ Often when people try this meditation for the first time, waves of objections often surface in their mind. The first one is: "But the door isn't getting any bigger, that's just my *perception* of the door as I get closer and closer." We have such a strong habit of looking at the world a certain way that it is hard at first to even see another way of viewing. But get this: there is no door other than your perception of a door. What other kind of door could there be?

◇ Another objection that inevitably comes up is. "But the door has to be the solid thing it is, because I can *feel* it." Let's look into this one a little bit.

◇ We establish the existence of things through touch as well as sight, but what exactly are we feeling? What can the hand feel?

◇ The hand cannot feel a door any more than the eye could see a door. The hand feels hardness, a bit of roughness here, some smooth curvy spot there, and then—just as the mind does with the data it gets from the eye—the mind pieces all these different tactile sensations together and calls them "door."

◊ The mind is so good at all of this interpretation process that it seamlessly links the information you are getting from your eye together with the data you are receiving from your sense of touch.

◊ Close your eyes and touch the door. The hand feels something hard, something smooth. Now open your eyes and look—the eye sees something brown that's shaped like a big rectangle. Do these two sets of things have anything in common?

◊ In itself, there is no connection at all between "rectangular, brown" and "hard, smooth." It is all the mind, taking random bits of input and creating one whole solid thing, which it then calls a "door."

◊ We'll try another, deeper version of this meditation, using the sense of feeling instead of sight, and our own body as the outer object.

MEDITATION

Your Body is Emptiness, Emptiness is Your Body

◇ Get into a comfortable position and then fix the body still.

◇ Turn your mind to the tip of your nose for a few minutes, just watching the air flow out and in.

◇ Now, focus on your body. Get a clear picture of it in your mind, as a whole.

◇ Go through each part of your body, one by one, from your toes all the way up to your head. At each part of the body, stop for a moment and feel it. Try and get a single-pointed focus on just that part alone, at each step.

◇ Think about how, when you were focusing on one part, you couldn't feel the rest of the body at all, if your focus was single-pointed. This process is a slowed-down version of what the mind does all day long to create your body. You can never feel the whole body all at once. You are just feeling parts, and then the mind is synthesizing those separate experiences together and calling them a "body."

◇ Where are your big toes when you are single-pointedly focused on your shoulder? Check. When you are not thinking about a particular part, you are no longer feeling it.

◇ That is because our big toes are not "out there" as we thought they were. If they were "out there," we would always feel them. They would never disappear when we were focused on something else.

◇ Focus again on your body as a whole.

◇ Try now to get a sense of your body being nothing but a mental image. Picture how your mind is projecting it—how it is not "out there," but coming from a tiny image in the back of your mind.

◇ What happens when you take that mental image away? What is left? You should be left with no body at all. Because the only body that exists is the body you are projecting.

◇ Keep going through these steps until you start to get a visceral feeling that there really isn't any body out there like you thought.

◇ Now think: what does it mean that the body I thought I had is not really out there? It means that all the problems and pains and aging which go along with having this body are not really out there either—they are all just a projection of my mind.

◇ Now practice re-imaging your body as completely perfect in every way, as we did in the angel meditation.

◇ Compare the two mental images: the one you normally have of your body and the one you are creating new. Both are coming from the mind—both are made of the same stuff. The only difference is, one you are projecting as "real" and one as "imagined."

◇ Think about the seeds you need to plant to see your imagined body as the real one.

36
Who Am I?

One of the most important things to know in your study of emptiness is that the day you see emptiness directly, it will be your own emptiness that you see. So we must start to explore now not just the emptiness of the objects around us but also the emptiness of our own selves.

When we say the word *self*, as in *me*, *myself*, who exactly are we talking about? Philosophers throughout the ages have spent entire lifetimes asking themselves that very question—Who am I?

We normally think of ourselves as the combination of our body and our mind. So let's examine this: am I my body?

Well, when someone touches it, we say: "I feel you," and when it goes without sleep, then we say: "I am tired." On the other hand, I can control my body. I can remember staying up all night on many occasions in college, against all desires of my body for sleep, in order to finish a term paper. So if the "I" is the controller of this body, how can I be my body?

So am I my mind?

What exactly is the mind? There is the constant stream of thoughts and feelings. There is the mind's power of discrimination—its ability to tell red from blue, left from right, good from bad. There is the ability to think and reason. All of these fall under the category of mind, but in Tibet there is a simpler definition. They say: the mind is "clear and aware."

Clear means that it has no quality of its own, but is able to take on the quality of any object it comes into contact with. So it is like a clear crystal. What happens when you take a red rose and put it beneath this crystal? When you look down at the crystal, it appears red. They say the mind is colored by the objects it sees. We'll cover this more in the next chapter.

But the essential word here is *aware*. The very most basic quality of the mind is awareness itself—being aware of what you see, hear, feel, smell, taste, or think. So is this *me*? Or is the whole combination of thoughts and feelings and so on "me?"

One thing to know about the mind is that it too is constantly changing. Our thoughts and feelings, they come and go like clouds moving across a blue sky. The powers of reasoning and discrimination surface and recede as well, as they are needed. Even our awareness is a moment-to-moment act of being.

There must be something behind all of it, right? Something deeper that is the driving force of both the body and mind.

There are certain schools of thought in ancient India that posit some kind of unchanging self deep within, that is beyond either body or mind—what we in the West might call a soul. But if you actually go and try and look for this thing, it is something you'll never find. In fact, it is completely impossible. For how could an unchanging thing ever interact with something that changes?

We all think this way. We all think that there is some kind of solid, real me beneath it all—someone unchanging, and in control. And we are all wrong.

Let's look into this "me" who is the owner of a body and a mind. An *owner* of something means the one in control of that thing. But do we control this body of ours? We think that we decide how this body moves—when I tell my arm to lift up, it does. Mostly. But there will come a day when you can no longer get your arm to lift. And constantly we are experiencing some kind of pain or discomfort in our bodies. If we were the boss of our bodies, we'd be able to tell it to stop hurting us, and it would comply.

It is even the same with the thoughts in our mind. Do you decide what thoughts you are going to have throughout the day? If we could decide that, then we'd all just decide to have only happy thoughts all the time. No, we are not even in control of the thoughts in our own mind as they surface. So who *is* thinking those thoughts, if it is not me? They are being projected by that other guy—the you of the past. The thoughts in our mind are mental imprints ripening exactly like the rest of the world. They are all made of the same stuff; they are all equally projections.

So who is this "me" if it is not the controller of my body or my mind? When we speak of these things, we say "my body" or "my mind" as if the "me" were something over and above these two things, something separate in nature from either body or mind. But what else could there be?

There *is* no fixed, separate "me" that exists apart from your body and mind—there is no director who is behind the scene in control of the whole show. There is nothing but the discrete moments of awareness we are having at any given time, and which we string together to call our mind.

Who is the "me" then that we are constantly referring to? It is nothing but an idea—a mere concept of the mind.

Seeing how the "me" that we thought was there doesn't even exist gets us one step closer to understanding how our entire perception of ourselves is empty. It too is just a constantly shifting projection, and thus it is completely possible for it to shift to an experience of a "me" filled with perfect bliss and wisdom.

MEDITATION

Looking for the Me

◇ Get into a comfortable position, and then lock the body still.

◇ Focus on your breath for a few moments, to calm the mind, watching the air flow out and then back in.

◇ Now go on a search, to try to find a fixed solid "me."

◇ Is "me" my body?

◇ Think first about how the body is constantly changing, getting older by the minute. It is not at all the same body as it was a year ago.

◇ Then think about what the body is made of—how it comes from so many other sources.

◇ How can this constantly changing thing that is composed entirely of foreign substances be me?

◇ Explore the mind—look at your constantly changing thoughts and feelings. Watch them as they rise and fade.

◇ How could this constantly changing experience be me?

◇ So if I am not my body, and I am not my mind, who am I?

◇ Next, call to mind your mistaken perception of a solid unchanging self—a me who is underneath this constantly shifting body and mind; a me who controls them.

◇ Think about how the body experiences pains that are beyond your control, and how it functions without your consent.

◇ How could it be *my* body if I can't control it?

◇ Again watch the constant flow of thoughts in the mind, and ask yourself where they are coming from. Think about how you have no present control when this mind gets upset or causes you pain.

◇ How could it be *my* mind if I can't control it?

◇ Start to get the feeling that there *is* no director of the body and mind underneath it all—that this me you always thought existed is simply a fabrication of your mind.

◇ Explore the feeling of absence you get as you realize the me that you always believed in is a me that does not exist.

37

Non-Duality

There is a museum in Amsterdam that I once went to, filled with all the works of the famous artist Van Gogh. I walked into the room, and there on the walls were dozens of his self-portraits, the same painting of Mr. Van Gogh's face on the canvas, over and over. They creatively titled them "Self Portrait #18," "Self Portrait #23," and so on. And I thought to myself, "Why did he paint so many portraits of his own face, and why on earth did he become famous for it?"

Then I looked closer. In each portrait, Van Gogh is wearing a different expression. In one, he is stern, as if scolding a child. In another, he is wounded, as if fighting with a lover. And suddenly it dawned on me what he was doing—through his own face, he was painting portraits of all the different people he knew. Wow, brilliant.

Now as I looked at each new painting, I could see the whole story there, encased in each expression. In each expression I could see the object he was looking at.

Van Gogh understood something about non-duality.

There is a subject: "me," and then there is the object that this *me* interacts with. And they are inexorably linked.

In Tibetan, the word for the subject state of mind is literally: "the thing that holds the object." There simply cannot be a subject without a corresponding object that it is holding onto.

Think about it: how do we interact with the things in our world? Through one of our sense consciousnesses—our eyes, ears, nose, mouth, tactile sense, or our mind. We see it, hear it, smell it, taste it, touch it, or think it, and that's how we confirm that an object exists.

Without a seer, there can be no seen thing. How could red exist without anyone to see it? Likewise, the seer couldn't be called a seer unless he was seeing something. Would an eye be an eye if it couldn't see? Thus the seer and the seen thing have a relationship of mutual dependence—each is necessary for the other's existence. The Tibetans call this "dependent origination."

So in one moment we are looking at something, and our visual consciousness is our subject state of mind. Then in the next moment we are listening to something, and our auditory consciousness is the subject. The moment after that, we are thinking of something, and our mental consciousness is the subject. When I say subject state of mind, what it means is the you of the moment. We already talked about how everything changes, moment to moment, and we got rid of any idea of a fixed, solid you back in the last chapter, so you have some understanding of how you yourself are constantly changing. You are going from being the seer to the hearer to the thinker, as each passing moment flashes by.

Try to catch the feeling, now, as you sit here. Could the you of the present moment—the one who is reading these words, right now— exist without your object? Could you exist without the words on this page? In your mind you are thinking: what a silly question! Of course I can—I can put down this book right now and focus on something entirely different.

But then that would be another moment, a different you. And *that* you would be connected to a different object.

Here's how that works: for every passing moment, a different karmic seed is ripening. And as it ripens, it produces an *experience*: both your experience of the world at that moment, *and* your experience of yourself at that moment. It is one whole package deal.

But during the ripening process, something happens—the experience splits into subject and object, and in our ignorance we see them as two totally separate things, things that have nothing to do with each other.

You think that the grumpy face across from you has nothing to do with your own state of mind at that moment. But in reality, your karmic seed created both the experiencer and the object experienced. So really, you are staring into you own face—the you of the present moment.

Watch the you of the present moment as it writes the words you read on this page.

Or look up, and lock onto a different object of experience, and watch yourself change.

Every single moment of experience is simply another changing moment of mind.

MEDITATION

Mahamudra–
The Diamond Realm of Mind

◇ Take a comfortable seat, and fix your body still.

◇ Focus for a few moments on your breath, to get the mind settled.

◇ As you focus on the breath, relax your control of the breath, so that the body breathes automatically, and you are simply watching it.

◇ Start to get a clear feeling of being simply the watcher. Cultivate a state of mind where you are in the back seat, and someone else is driving.

◇ Now, take this same watcher state of mind, and turn it to your thoughts. Relax and let the thoughts rise at will—you are no longer the thinker, you are simply watching whatever arises.

◇ Whenever any thought or picture surfaces in the mind, be careful not to grasp onto it or let yourself fall into that thought. Keep yourself at a distance, as the watcher, and simply observe.

◇ Observe how each thought or picture rises from a state of nothingness, and then dissipates back into nothing.

◇ Next, observe how with each passing thought, your awareness is colored by the object it is focused on.

◇ See how the watcher arises together with each passing object of thought. See how the watcher too is just a moment-to-moment karmic ripening. There is no fixed, solid awareness; there is only the moment of experience.

◇ Then as you watch, turn your mind to emptiness— see each and every passing thought or picture that arises as lacking any real substance—nothing but a ripple on the surface of your awareness, nothing but a moment of mind.

◇ As you hold this watcher state of mind, the ripples of thought start to fade. Concentrate then on the space between the thoughts. Explore that silence.

◇ Ask yourself a question then: what is awareness without any object to be aware of? What is a watcher without anything to watch?

◇ Focus the mind then on the emptiness of the watcher itself—how your very awareness is nothing but a moment-to-moment ripening, with no real nature of its own.

◇◇◇

There is another meaning of non-duality that you often find in the ancient texts, and that is a synonym for seeing emptiness directly.

When we enter into the direct perception of emptiness, we go beyond all conceptual thought. There are no more objects of the senses—nothing to see, hear, smell, taste, feel, or think of.

And there are no more powers of sense—no seeing, hearing, smelling, tasting, feeling, or even thinking. There is no more you, because you are a concept. When you are immersed in the direct perception of emptiness, there is no subject state of mind, and no object that it holds.

Does that mean you disappear—that you no longer exist? Not exactly. The text sometimes describes it as "water poured into water"—undifferentiatable, subject and object inseparably joined together, no longer divided, non-dual.

38

The Power Of Words

> "In the beginning was the word."
> — The Bible, John 1:1

> "The word is indeed the word
> And it is far beyond any normal thing."
> — Tao te Ching, Master Lao Tzu

We already have some idea of the power of words. We have seen great countries built from and wars fought over two tiny little words *democracy* and *communism*. These are concepts, mere ideas in the mind that do not have any kind of reality in the outside world. And yet how they function!

The entire world runs like that. Everything is resting on the power of words, of names, of ideas. All the "things" we ever meet, including that object called you, are made from words. The word comes first, and everything else follows.

Of course when I say "word," I don't mean a sound that you hear, or some letters printed on a page. We are talking about the mental image or idea behind those things—the tiny pictures in the back of the mind that are the foundation for all your projections.

Say for instance you are sitting in the front of a table in your three-year retreat. It is a squat little thing made of three pieces of yellow wood—the thing you use to place the one book you are allowed to read upon in front of you on the floor, so that you can do your daily visualization and recitation. You are staring at this little guy in front of you, and wondering, "why am I seeing a table?" And suddenly it dawns on you—there is no table out there; it is just a little word in my mind.

Think about it: what do tables look like? When I say the word "table," what kind of image pops up in your mind? It will be different for everyone. For me, the image that comes up when I think "table" is the dining room table I had when I was growing up—a thick, round piece of dark brown wood resting on four tall legs, that could be pulled apart in the middle and a piece added to make it slightly bigger when guests come over. Now, if that is what a table looks like, how in the world did I ever think that this squat little yellow thing sitting in front of me was a table? What about it gave me the first clue? It's not tall, in fact it is only about a foot and a half high. It is not dark brown, nor is it round. In fact, it looks absolutely nothing like a table should. So why is it a table to me?

People will now say—because I am using it as a table. Ah, but in order to use something as a table, you have to first have the idea to use it as a table, and in order to have that idea, you must see it as a table. The picture always comes first.

I like going to museums on occasion and seeing some of the things people have dug up, from centuries ago. When the archeologists don't know what something is, they simply label it "decorative item." Now imagine someone far in the future digging up my little yellow thing, labeling it "decorative item," and hanging it on a wall somewhere. It is not a table from its side—nothing about it says "table" to someone who looks at it.

There is a word, a concept, a tiny idea in the back of my mind. It is the word "table." And it gets projected onto the yellow thing in front of me, so that I think I am seeing a table. But there are no tables. There is only "table." And that's why I can use it as a table.

MEDITATION

Word vs. Thing

◇ Get into a comfortable seat, let your eyes fall closed, and still the body.

◇ Focus on your breath for a few minutes, and let the mind too fall still.

◇ Think about the concept or idea "table." Try and get in touch with the little word in the back of your mind—the one that makes you understand the letters "t-a-b-l-e," the one responsible for all the tables you ever saw.

◇ Now think about how "table" relates to a table or the table. "Table" is a blanket idea that encompasses all the tables you ever saw. And a table, in turn, is a thing which resembles "table". You could also say that a table has the quality of tableness.

◇ Where does this tableness come from? Is it in the table itself? No, it is inside the word "table"—that tiny idea in the back of your mind.

◇ Now think: have you ever actually seen a table? Or have you been looking at "table" all along?

◇ Find the gakja—get a sense of absence as you find the table that you thought was there, the table that doesn't exist at all.

◇ Do this same meditation using any other object.

39

The Raw Data

But what's really out there? What is the raw data that I am projecting my little image "table" onto? That would be the three yellow pieces of wood. But then, if you go looking for these pieces of wood, you realize that they are not out there either.

"Wood" is a concept. The eye cannot see "wood" any more than the hand could feel it. We covered this before with the door. The mind is taking the idea "wood" and projecting it onto some rectangular yellow things.

But what about the yellow rectangles? Are they out there? Tibetan scriptures always say: if you don't delve into a thing, it appears to be there. But once you start looking for the thing, you'll never ever find it.

Once the raw data itself becomes the object of your emptiness exploration, then it too becomes merely a projection labeled onto its own raw data. In this case, your mind is taking edges and corners and pieces of yellow that the eye sees millisecond to millisecond, and piecing it all together to form a rectangular object. Really the eye can't see "rectangle" either. It too is a concept, a word.

So in the end, what does the eye really see? Nothing. It sees nothing at all.

If our eyes worked the way we thought they did, it would be impossible for them to see anything. For how could a seer—something with a fixed nature of seeing—ever stop seeing long enough to see an object? That one is difficult—I think you'll have to cook it a bit.

So what's actually happening?   The object and the eye consciousness are arising together—a projection of the same karmic seed ripening. Sight itself is just a concept, just another idea in the mind.

MEDITATION

Infinite Parts

◇ Get into a comfortable position, fix your body still.

◇ Take a few minutes to focus on your breath, watch the air flow out and in.

◇ Turn your focus again to your body. See how the mind is creating this idea of "body" out of all the disparate parts that you feel.

◇ Now we will check and see: are those parts themselves really there?

◇ Focus on your left hand. Get a clear feeling and picture of it in your mind.

◇ See now how it too is composed of many parts that you would have to feel one by one: each part of the fingers, the palm, the back of the hand.

◇ So the mind must also be taking all these disparate parts and gathering them together to create the concept of "a hand."

◇ "Hand" is not really out there—it is just an idea in the mind, superimposed over several different moments of experience.

◇ Now focus on one of those parts—your left index finger.

◇ See how many parts of its own it has. See how you have to experience these parts one by one. The top of the finger, up to the first crease, the joint, the base, the front, the back.

◇ So "left index finger" is really just a concept of the mind, created by gathering together moments of experience, overlaying an image onto disparate parts.

◇ What about the tip of the finger? Can you feel each separate part? It too would have to be pasted together from all its disparate parts. It too is a concept.

◇ Then think: you can take a part of the tip of the finger and divide that too into separate moments of experience. In fact, you could keep on dividing like this, infinitely.

◇ So ask yourself this question: how are you feeling all those parts of parts of parts of the body in time for the mind to synthesize them all together and see or feel a body?

◇ You're not! It's impossible. And that's one proof that the body you see and feel right now is not out there— it is just an image coming from your mind.

40
Nothing Ever Touches

Does the tree touch the sky?
—Geshe Michael Roach

If there is not one, how could there be many?
—Arya Nagarjuna

So everything we see is simply a projection—
so things have no nature of their own. Then
why do things function? Why does my car
get me to work? Why can a flame light a
stick of incense? If things really didn't
have any nature—if my car didn't have the
nature of getting me from place to place—
then couldn't the flame just as well get me
to work?

Your car isn't the cause of getting
you to work. And the simple proof of
that is that sometimes people get
in their car, but never make it to
work. If something is a cause
for something else, it should
always bring the same result.

The real cause for getting where you want to go is having helped other people get where they wanted to go in the past.

Picture how one thing causes another—you hold the tip of a stick of incense over a flame from your lighter for a second, and then pull it away. The moment after, smoke starts to rise from the tip of the stick. So we say: the fire *caused* the smoke. Is it true? Can one thing ever cause another?

The fire comes first, and then the smoke comes a moment later— *after the fire is already gone*. But if something is the cause of something else, wouldn't it have to have some kind of connection to the result? Wouldn't cause and result have to interact; wouldn't they have to touch?

Does the last moment of the flame touch the first moment of the smoke? Can you find the point in time where they meet? Maybe there's a fraction of a second? Picture it. But that fraction of a second has a beginning and an end to it, right? So really that is not the actual point where they meet. Divide that fraction until you find the real point in time where they meet. Did you find it? But that infinitesimal moment in time too has a beginning and an end.

Are you starting to see? You can never *find* the point in time when the two of cause and result actually meet, because the divisions are endless.

This is the same for anything that supposedly interacts. See now the physical point where the flame first touches the tip of the stick. Can you find it? The very first point where the two make contact. How big is this point? If you can see it, it must have some width to it. It has a front and a back end. So it must not be the real point where they touch. Divide it into a smaller point... and so on, and so on. You can never find the very first point where two things touch. And if there's no first point, how could there ever be a second?

Fire doesn't have any nature of making things burn. Because the fire is not out there, existing from its own side like you thought it was. The fire is just a picture in your mind, and that picture is what makes things burn.

So yes, if you had a different set of pictures in your mind, your lighter *could* get you to work in the morning.

Anything is possible, because of emptiness.

41
Projection

During deep states of retreat, you start to have what the Tibetans call "lucid dreams." This is like dreaming but being so aware that you are dreaming that it feels as if you're awake. I was having one of these kinds of dreams sometime during the 3-year retreat. And in this particular dream, I was translating a Tibetan text—one I didn't remember ever seeing before.

Now this itself was a common enough thing for me to be doing, as it is what I spend a good part of my time on. However, because I knew I was dreaming, I had this strange awareness that my mind was actually creating the Tibetan text as I was reading it. But here's the funny thing: sometimes it takes me hours to translate even a single page of Tibetan. I honestly haven't had the drive to learn the Tibetan language well enough to actually write in Tibetan. Yet there was this book...a beautiful masterpiece of Tibetan scripture, created by my own mind in my dream. And I was watching my mind create it.

This is exactly what is happening in our waking world. Our minds are creating things that are far beyond our conscious self to grasp, all the time. Our mind creates the road as we drive down the street. It makes the stairs, one by one, as we step on them. It makes the words as you read a book.

It is painting the picture of the world, and then painting itself within it, every single moment.

There are only two things: the projection, and that which lies beyond it.

Think about the door again. Can you walk to the door? No, because there is no space between you and the door, and there is no time it takes to walk across the room to get there. All movement is an illusion—there is only peace: just now, and now, and now.

Can you walk to the door? No, because there is no you, and there is no door. Withdraw all the elaborations, and come to rest in the sublime quiet that words cannot express.

VI.

Gyu:
The Way of the Secret

42

A Taste of Tantra

So that is emptiness, but how do we use it?

Once you start to understand emptiness even just a little, you begin to get a taste of the immense power behind it. Think about it: there is no "real world"; there is nothing out there besides what I am projecting. It is all coming from me. And that means, it could be anything, given the right set of mental imprints. And this body and mind that make up "me," they too are nothing but projections. That means I too could be anything, anything at all.

And so we reach now an understanding of the inseparable nature of karma and emptiness. They are two sides of the same coin: everything is a projection, and nothing is not; everything is completely absent of any inherent existence, and nothing I ever experience is anything other than the ripening of mental imprints planted by my own past actions.

So on one level, we could use our understanding of emptiness to prevent collecting negative karma and thus prevent negative things from happening. For instance, if someone yells at you, you remember where that unpleasant seed is coming from and you don't yell back, thereby preventing this unpleasant circumstance from happening in the future.

But we can also go a step further, and use our understanding of emptiness in a more active way, by consciously collecting karmic seeds. For instance, we could consciously work on being generous, in order to see our financial status change for the better.

This second way of using emptiness is the basis of the higher practices of Tibetan Buddhism. There are good karmic seeds, and then there are powerfully good karmic seeds. And since this life we have is rather short, why waste time collecting the small goodnesses when you can be collecting the seeds to stop death itself, in this very life?

This is where tantra comes in.

What is tantra?

Tantra is the collection of highest teachings of Tibetan Buddhism—the teachings that must be passed down orally in the proper way from teacher to student, the teachings that require years of preparation to practice, the teachings you simply cannot learn from a book. These are the teachings in which we learn about the fastest karmic methods of changing our body and our mind. And of course I cannot tell you everything here, for as one of my Lamas always used to say, "Tantra means secret!"

The Tibetans, however, have always believed in the power of planting seeds. So here now is just a taste of your practice to come.

43

Suspension of Disbelief

Take yourself back to the last time you saw a good movie. What do you remember the most? Were you really impressed with the lighting technique, or the superb ability of the main character? I hope not! If it was a really good movie, it swept you away in the story so much that you forgot you were even watching something unreal.

This is a process those in the acting business like to call "suspension of disbelief"—you as an audience member agree to temporarily forget all about the cameras and the set and the crew and how much money it cost to make it, and just let yourself believe in the story.

Since we in these modern times are such active movie goers, we are already quite adept at one of the most basic skills you need to practice the higher teachings— believing in the story.

What is the story? It is a story about you, and about the world around you. It is a fairytale you decide to believe in, that plants the seeds in your mind to see it actually come true.

44

Looking for Angels

Once you reach the ultimate goal, and become yourself what the Tibetans call an enlightened Being, you are instantly transported to heaven.

Where do you go? Nowhere. The seeds in your mind simply… shift, and you see everyone in the world around you as totally pure.

How do they see themselves? It depends on their own karmic seeds. Does that mean you are not seeing their real nature? Come on, nothing has any real nature, we just went over that.

So you see them as angels, but you also have the ability to read their minds and see how they perceive themselves in pain. And your totally perfect, pure heart is filled with love and compassion for them, and you long to help them.

So you emanate. You send out bodies of yourself, in whatever different form their karma would allow them so see. (For you see, not everyone can see a shining Being of pure light.) You stay with them—in that form, or in another if it is helpful—and push them in the right direction until they reach the goal.

This is the nature of enlightened Beings. Their emanations are countless. It is what They most love to do all day, every day. It gives Them incredible bliss (but of course, everything does).

Consider this. If it is true that enlightened Beings exist, if it is true that They love us, and if it is true that They have the power to emanate—it is absolutely certain that They are emanating in some form or another for you, right now.

Who is it? Who in your life is the enlightened Being in disguise? Your mom, your partner, your child?

Could there be more than one?

What if everybody but me is already enlightened?

You don't know for sure. You can't read their minds.

We have this habit of looking at the people around us as normal—as someone like ourselves—without any proof at all that this is the case.

But who wants to live in a world full of "normal" people?

Write a different story.

MEDITATION

Believing

◇ Settle into a comfortable position, then relax and let the body fall still.

◇ Focus on your breath for a few minutes to calm the mind, just watching the air flow out and back in.

◇ Let your mind reflect for a minute on all the people you come into contact with on a regular basis—the people who form the circle of your daily life.

◇ Think about the story you have built up about this circle surrounding you— how you believe that they are simply "normal" people.

◇ Now, create a different story—allow yourself to entertain the possibility that these are all in fact enlightened Beings in disguise, here to help you.

◇ Think about some of the things these Beings have said or done to you recently that have guided you or pointed you in the right direction.

◇ Now think about the last argument you got into with one of these Beings, and figure out how that as well was all purposely designed to help you on your journey to enlightenment.

◇ In closing, try to plan some moment during your day when you stop and remember this meditation—some moment where you look around suspiciously at all the so-called "normal" people surrounding you.

◇ This meditation actually plants the seed for you yourself to become an Angel—an enlightened Being—for you are practicing seeing the world as you will see it when you reach the final stage of your evolution.

◇ Another way to practice though, is simply to sit and envision yourself as the Angel, with a body of light and a pure, perfect mind, just as we did in the very first meditation in this book

45
The Inner Body of an Angel

Do you have to die to reach an Angel's body? Of course not. This decaying, worn out old physical body we have is nothing but a projection—a projection that could change in an instant, to an entirely new kind of body.

Is this new body physical? Yes, it is made of a very subtle form of physical material—stuff that is finer than light.

We have these same subtle substances within us already, running deep inside our gross physical body. These substances are the raw material that will become the Angel's form.

There are inner channels within the body, stretching out like nerves to every corner inside us. They are made of something like light, and they carry our inner winds.

The inner winds are called lung in Tibetan, chi in Chinese, or prana in Sanskrit. Perhaps you've heard of them by one of these names.

On the winds ride our thoughts; they are the physical counterpart of every mental activity. Right now, our thoughts are mistaken because our winds are running through the wrong channels. Or is it that right now our winds are running through the wrong channels because our thoughts are mistaken? Again, it is simply two sides of the same coin.

Get the winds into the channel in the center, and you will see emptiness directly. Get the winds to stay in this channel, and you won't have to die.

MEDITATION

Into the Center

◇ Take a comfortable position, then relax and let the body fall still.

◇ Focus on the breath for a few moments, watching the air pass out and then back into your body.

◇ Turn your mind to your physical form. Picture it as nothing but a hollow shell— the outside made of light, and the inside completely empty and clear, like the clear blue sky.

◇ Travel inside your body from the top of your head to the tip of your toes, making sure that there is nothing inside but sky blue clear space.

◇ Now, in the space where your backbone used to be, picture a hollow tube made of red light, running from the center tip of your head down to your tailbone. It is the width of a straw, shining and translucent.

◇ Go deep inside this tube—become the wind that runs within it.

◇ Try to listen for the song of this wind as it courses through the central channel.

46
Ending, and Beginning

This concludes the Tibetan Book of Meditation. But in Tibet, a book is not something you read once and then put away on your shelf to collect dust. It is something you treasure, something that you will take out and use again and again.

So go now—go and sit and meditate. Take this with you as a guide on your journey, let this knowledge be your lifetime friend. Change the world with it, and let it change yourself. We will meet face to face sooner or later, and when we do, I am looking forward to seeing the person you will become.

Dedication

By the truth of the inseparable pair
Of emptiness and karma,

By the power
Of my pure intent
In writing out these teachings

May everyone who reads it
Find meditative stillness

And may they then go on to see
Emptiness directly

May this vision clear away
Every last mistaken thought

And then may they go on to reach
The Union of the Two

For further information, or to hear the audio versions of these meditations, go to tibetanbookofmeditation.org.